THE
NEW WAVE
OF
JAPANESE
INVESTMENT
IN
ASEAN

The **Institute of Southeast Asian Studies** (ISEAS) was established as an autonomous organization in 1968. It is a regional research centre for scholars and other specialists concerned with modern Southeast Asia, particularly the many-faceted problems of stability and security, economic development, and political and social change.

The Institute is governed by a twenty-two-member Board of Trustees comprising nominees from the Singapore Government, the National University of Singapore, the various Chambers of Commerce, and professional and civic organizations. A ten-man Executive Committee oversees day-to-day operations; it is chaired by the Director, the Institute's chief academic and administrative officer.

The **ASEAN Economic Research Unit** is an integral part of the Institute, coming under the overall supervision of the Director who is also the Chairman of its Management Committee. The Unit was formed in 1979 in response to the need to deepen understanding of economic change and political developments in ASEAN. The day-to-day operations of the Unit are the responsibility of the Coordinator. A Regional Advisory Committee, consisting of a senior economist from each of the ASEAN countries, guides the work of the Unit.

THE NEW WAVE OF JAPANESE INVESTMENT IN ASEAN

DETERMINANTS AND PROSPECTS

Pasuk Phongpaichit
Chulalongkorn University

ASEAN Economic Research Unit
INSTITUTE OF SOUTHEAST ASIAN STUDIES

This publication was produced with a subsidy from the Japan Foundation, Tokyo.

Published by
Institute of Southeast Asian Studies
Heng Mui Keng Terrace
Pasir Panjang
Singapore 0511

The responsibility for facts and opinions expressed in this publication rests exclusively with the author and her interpretations do not necessarily reflect the views or the policy of the Institute or its supporters.

Cataloguing in Publication Data

Pasuk Phongpaichit.
　The new wave of Japanese investment in ASEAN : determinants and prospects.
　1.　Investments, Japanese -- ASEAN countries.
　I.　Institute of Southeast Asian Studies (Singapore)
HG5740.8 A3P29　　　1990　　　sls90-35096

ISBN 981-3035-62-5

Printed in Singapore by Denko Press Pte Ltd

Contents

Acknowledgements

I carried out this study while holding a Research Fellowship at the Institute of Southeast Asian Studies in 1988 and 1989. I am greatly indebted to the Institute, and especially to Professor Kernial S. Sandhu, for encouragement and support.

I would like to extend my thanks to all those who have helped me in the course of my research including: Dr Narongchai Akrasanee, Dr Joseph Tan Loong Hoe, Shoko Sasaki, Keiko Chida, Hirayuki Shimamura, Dr Lysa Hong, Ahmad D. Habir, Dr Hadi Susastro, Dr Mari Pangestu, Dr Hal Hill, Dr M.K. Chng, Professor Stephen Chee, Dr Norbert Wagner, Thee Kian Wee, Dr Djisman Simanjuntak, Dr Toh Kin Woon, Tan Sri Datuk Hamzah Sendut, Professor S. Hirashima, Seiki Teshiba, Masuyuki Sueda, Takeshi Mori, Takashi Torii, Akiko Akemine, Yakata Harada, Dr Mukul Asher, and the anonymous readers for the Institute of Southeast Asian Studies.

I would also like to thank the Faculty of Economics, Chulalongkorn University for allowing me to take up the Research Fellowship at the Institute. Finally I must thank Chris Baker, who put up with impromptu debates at unlikely times, and who also helped with the editing. Any shortcomings of this study are entirely my own.

ISEAS, Singapore
September 1989

1

Introduction

In the late 1980s, foreign direct investment, and in particular Japanese direct investment, became a major factor in the ASEAN economies. In the earlier part of the decade, this was barely foreseen. Investment from the West was declining, especially as the United States, the major Western investor country of the past, had recently been transformed into the world's largest debtor nation. Japanese firms were creating labour-saving and energy-saving technologies, and moving back to Japan some of the labour and energy intensive processes which had earlier been relocated overseas.

The change has been rapid. In the three years from 1985 to 1987 Japanese direct investment in ASEAN totalled over US$3.3 billion. This compared to a total flow of US$12.5 billion over the previous three decades.[1] Foreign investment still represents a relatively minor percentage of total domestic investment in most ASEAN states (Singapore is the exception). Yet it is widely acknowledged that Japanese direct investment is playing an increasingly more important role because it is concentrated in the new, higher-tech, export-oriented industries which are powering the high growth rates of several ASEAN states. And it is expected to remain an important force for several years in the future.

This is a study of the forces driving the "new wave"[2] of Japanese foreign investment in ASEAN. The study is confined to investment in manufacturing. Although investment in services is becoming more important, it is not covered here because of a lack of adequate information. The study does not attempt to assess the impact which this investment is making on the ASEAN economies. Since the new wave is relatively recent, and many projects are still at the gestation stage, it is too early to assess the impact in a meaningful way. Rather it is a study of the determinants and the determining characteristics of this new phase of Japanese overseas investment. In order to evaluate the impact of this new wave, in order to predict its future course, and in order to be able to craft policies to manage it with maximum benefit for the host economies, we first need to understand the forces which are driving and shaping the flow of the new investment.

Although this is a study of Japanese direct investment, we must bear in mind that Japan is but one among many players in the region. Foreign investment inflow into the region now involves several investor countries, and is to some extent competitive. In the past five years, investment from the Asian newly industrializing countries (NICs) of Taiwan, Korea and Hong Kong has increased even more dramatically than that from Japan, and by 1988 in some ASEAN countries the combined investment from these three states exceeded that from Japan. However, Japan is still the single largest overseas investor in ASEAN. By focusing solely on Japanese investment, we can claim to be focusing on the most important element of foreign investment.

The study covers the four countries of Indonesia, Malaysia, Singapore and Thailand, which together account for over 95 per cent of the total flow of Japanese investment into ASEAN in the period 1985–87. The study does not extend to the Philippines, which accounted for less than 5 per cent of the total inflow, or Brunei, which accounted for an insignificant amount. In the future, it is probable that Japanese investment into the Philippines will increase. However, at this stage Japanese investment has focused on four countries in ASEAN and these countries have been chosen for this study.

This study has three main parts: a review of existing theoretical approaches to overseas investment and especially Japanese overseas investment; a study of supply side factors driving and shaping the flow of Japanese investment into ASEAN; and a study of demand side factors within the ASEAN host countries.

Chapter 2 contains a review of existing approaches to the study of overseas investment. It describes two main approaches. First, in the 1960s and 1970s, a number of Western-based economists approached the study of overseas investment through micro-economic analysis of the multinational firm. Second, beginning in the late 1970s, a number of Japanese economists used a macro-economic perspective based on comparative advantage to analyse the special nature of Japanese overseas investment. Both approaches focused heavily on the supply side — either the internal dynamic of the multinational firm, or the comparative advantage of the investor country. Following this review, an alternative approach with two major features is presented. First, the approach integrates micro-economic and macro-economic perspectives. Second, it introduces a framework for integrating the demand side into the analysis of determinants of foreign investment flows.

Chapter 3 examines the new wave of Japanese investment from the supply side. After describing the "old wave" of Japanese investment before the mid-1980s and indicating the scale and key differentiating characteristics of the new wave, the chapter focuses on two main developments which have shaped the new wave: first, the structural change of the Japanese economy and its relationship to the rest of the world, and second, the changing nature of the Japanese firm.

Chapter 4 uses the framework introduced at the end of Chapter 2 to analyse the demand for foreign investment in the ASEAN states. It argues that there are two key elements affecting the demand for foreign investment: first, the attitudes and strategies of host governments, and second, the attitudes and strategies of domestic capital. Then it uses a historical approach to describe how the demand for foreign investment changed from generally low in most ASEAN countries in the 1960s and 1970s, to much higher in the 1980s, especially from the mid-1980s onwards.

Chapter 5 summarizes the argument, and then uses the analytical approach to make outline predictions concerning the future course and likely impact of the new wave of Japanese investment in the ASEAN states. These predictions are then used to indicate key issues for policy-making.

Notes

1. Toru Nakakita, "The Globalisation of Japanese Firms and Its Influence on Japan's Trade and Developing Countries", *The Developing Economies* 26, no. 4 (1988): 308. But see qualification concerning these figures in Chapter 3 below.
2. I use the term "new wave" to refer to the period from 1985 onwards. The characteristics which differentiate the new wave from the old wave, extending from the mid-1950s to the mid-1980s, are discussed in Chapter 3 below.

2

Approaches to Japanese direct investment

The post-war phase of Japanese overseas investment began in the mid-1950s and rapidly grew in volume through the 1960s, especially within the Asian region. By the mid-1970s it had become large enough to become a political issue in several ASEAN states. By the end of the decade, the flow of investment funds from Japan exceeded the flow from the United States. Against this background, Japanese direct investment became a topic for academic study, both in the home and host countries.

In the 1960s and 1970s, analysis of overseas investment by Western economists had focused on the multinational firm, the major agent of overseas investment from the United States and elsewhere. The initial Japanese studies of Japanese overseas investment marked a deliberate departure from this approach. They explicitly rejected the micro-economic study of the firm in favour of a framework based on comparative advantage.

This chapter reviews three approaches to overseas investment. First, it briefly summarizes the major interests of Western economists concerned with the multinational firm. Second, it reviews the Japanese contribution, starting with the major work of Kojima, and continuing with criticisms of, and extensions to, this approach by other Japanese and non-Japanese economists. Third, it indicates the main trends of analysis in studies by economists from the host countries within ASEAN.

While differing widely in theoretical concerns and conclusions, all these approaches share one general aspect in common; they all focus heavily on determinants of the *supply* of foreign investment, and have neglected a general framework for the analysis of the *demand* for foreign investment. The final section of the chapter introduces a framework for integrating demand into the analysis.

Western approaches to the theory of foreign investment

Traditional trade theory treated foreign direct investment as a form of international movement of capital (Ohlin 1933). Differences in the relative factor endowment ratios of capital and labour among countries caused differences in the rate of return to capital as represented in the level of interest rates. This led to flows of capital from capital-rich to capital-poor countries. This view of foreign direct investment as capital movement proved to be inadequate in explaining foreign investment by developed countries. Empirically it was found that the majority of foreign direct investment was not directed towards countries which were poorly endowed with financial capital, but rather towards developed countries, and a large percentage of the capital expenditure of foreign subsidiaries was financed from local sources.

Noting that the key agent of recent (post World War II) Western foreign investment was the multinational firm, a number of Western economists in the 1960s and 1970s analysed foreign investment by applying industrial organization theory to the actions of the multinational firm. Their investigations began from the assumption that a multinational operating in a foreign country was faced with certain costs which local firms did not face. These costs arose from cultural differences, difficulties in understanding local language and markets, problems with bureaucracy and so on. To compensate for these disadvantages, multinational firms investing overseas had to have some countervailing advantages which enabled them to compete successfully against local rivals. The attention was thus turned on the specific advantages of the investing firms and the ways in which these advantages affected their strategy for corporate growth.

A pioneer among this group of economists was Hymer, who was the first to demonstrate that the central motive for direct investment was the firm's desire to control foreign operations. This direct control was necessary in order to obtain the full returns on advantages of skills and abilities which that firm possessed over local and foreign competitors (Hymer 1976).[1] These advantages could be of various kinds: access to cheap capital or raw materials; access to larger markets which led to economies of scale; exclusive possession of intangible assets such as managerial skills and superior technology; or the information, Research and Development (R&D) and other infrastructure available in the multinational network. Of all these, Hymer concluded that knowledge or technological advantage over local firms was the most important.

However, Hymer recognized that possession of technological advantage might not be a necessary condition for direct foreign investment, and other economists elaborated the argument further, arguing that imperfections in the markets were important additional factors which ensured that firms could exploit their specific advantages through discriminatory pricing (Kindleberger 1969; Caves 1971; Horst 1978). Caves and Horst argued that firms were induced to invest directly overseas when they possessed well-established brand names and other forms of product differentiation which created monopolistic advantages over local and other foreign firms. The marketing advantages of oligopolistic firms with differentiated products offset disadvantages inherent in investing and operating overseas, and could explain why these firms invested abroad. Caves also argued that large firms were in a better position to fund the large initial outlays involved in overseas operations, and thus he associated foreign direct investment with large oligopolistic firms.

The product cycle theory proposed by Raymond Vernon was a variant of the industrial organization approach to foreign investment (Vernon 1966, 1981; Wells 1972). It attempted to integrate the firm-specific advantages theory with the theory of international trade. It regarded technological innovation as the main determinant of the structure of world trade and of the distribution of production among different countries. Technological innovations were firm-specific advantages and the differentials in these assets gave rise to comparative advantage among firms in different locations. These comparative advantages explained patterns of trade and investment.

The product-cycle model comprised three stages. In the first stage a firm in an advanced country innovated a new product. As long as the technology for producing the product was not yet standardized, the production was located in the country of origin where there was a good supply of suitably skilled labour and easy access to the major market, and the originating firm enjoyed a monopolistic position in the market. In the second stage the production technology became more standardized, more firms entered the market, demand became price elastic, and firms competed with one another to improve productivity and realize economies of scale. With standardized technology, firms could mass-produce for export, or even relocate the production to countries with lower unskilled labour costs. In the final stage, firms were virtually obliged to relocate production to low-cost countries and import finished products back to the originating country, or face the prospect that competitors would relocate and steal the market. Thus according to the product cycle theory the move overseas was prompted initially by a desire to pre-empt other competitors from sharing in markets.[2]

For the industrial organization theorists, the key determinants of foreign investment were thus firm-specific advantages and the imperfections in the markets.

More recent works attempted to give a more precise definition of these firm-specific advantages.[3] Hennart argued that the key advantages arose from innovations in legal forms, organizational structure, management techniques and international communications. Firms which possessed these advantages found they could realize better profits by direct investment rather than by licensing ventures (Hennart 1982). Buckley and Casson (1976) added that there were certain advantages inherent in the multinationalism of the multinational firm. Through transfer pricing, vertical integration of production, and similar techniques, multinational firms could generate economies which raised the profitability of direct investment versus licensing or similar arrangements.[4]

Subsequently Casson identified the key advantage of the multinational firm as its ability to internalize the transaction costs associated with the development of R&D and the accumulation of knowledge. The more the firm could accumulate knowledge and R&D at low transaction costs, the greater would be the benefit it could realize from directly marketing the resulting products rather than simply selling the technology. In these circumstances, firms would choose to license technology only if host governments refused to allow direct investment (Casson 1987).

More recently, economists became interested in new forms of overseas involvement which differed from the conventional style of direct investment (Oman 1984). These forms included technology contracts, management contracts, franchise arrangements, turnkey projects and production sharing. These have been labelled as "new forms of investment". Oman categorized these new forms of operation into two main types. In the first, the foreign-held equity was usually less than 50 per cent. In the second, the foreign firm contributed no equity capital at all, but provided technology, expertise or brand name franchise in return for some management control and some long-term arrangement for compensation. This arrangement could be a long-term contract or grant of a minority equity share.

The new forms of investment involved some unbundling of the "package" of traditional foreign direct investment, which usually included equity or financial capital along with embodied or disembodied technology, management and even access to world markets. According to the industrial organization approach to overseas investment, these new forms appeared because multinational firms found them a more profitable way to optimize the return from their innovations and from their accumulated skills and knowledge in management and marketing compared to traditional equity participation (Chee 1989a). Small and medium sized firms which accumulated firm-specific advantages in small-scale production, unique technology or organization know-how might prefer the new form of investment as a means to get an optimal return to their specific advantages because they had limited financial and managerial resources (Chee 1989a).

Kojima and a "Japanese" model of foreign investment

The "organization", "transaction" and "product cycle" approaches to the analysis of foreign investment were all developed to help explain the behaviour of multinational corporations, and particularly American multinational corporations. In the 1960s, these multinationals were the major agents for overseas investment. From 1969 onwards, foreign investment began to flow out of Japan at an ever-increasing rate until by 1980 Japan overtook the United

States in terms of net annual outflow of investment. By the late 1970s, the analysis of foreign investment had become a topic of major importance for Japanese economists.[5]

Their approaches to the theory of foreign investment diverged sharply from the micro-economic concerns of Western theory. Among the Japanese approaches, the most remarkable was that of Kojima, not least because of his aggressive departure from Western theory.

Kojima argued that the product cycle theory and other approaches from micro-economic theory tended to explain the motivation to invest overseas in terms of the defence of monopolistic or oligopolistic advantages (Kojima 1973a, 1973b, 1978). He was concerned that this approach encouraged host countries to view foreign investment as exploitative and often directly antagonistic to the better interests of host country firms and the host economy as a whole. To counter this tendency, Kojima did not argue that the theory of monopolistic advantage was wrong, but rather that it was only one of a range of motivations for foreign investment. He went on to draw a contrast between American investments overseas, which often could be explained in terms of the defence of monopolistic or oligopolistic advantage, and Japanese investments which he claimed were differently motivated and more benignly complementary to the host country economy. To achieve this contrast, Kojima switched the approach away from the micro-economic perspective of organization theory, and back to the macro-economic framework of comparative advantage and the international division of labour.

Kojima (1978) elaborated his theoretical exposition, based on the well-known Heckscher-Ohlin theorem, in his book *The Theories of Foreign Investment*. He divided direct investment into four major types: resource-oriented, labour-oriented, market-oriented, and oligopolistic, and argued that each type had a different motivation, and a different impact on trade and on the host country economy.

Resource-oriented investment was undertaken to increase the production of natural resource products which the home country lacked. This type of investment generated trade, because it resulted from the home country's lack of comparative advantage and its desire to secure a supply of natural resource products from the host country. The investment thus increased exports of primary products from the host country to home and third countries. But where production and marketing were integrated within the same foreign multinational firm, host countries might receive small benefits in terms of returns because of the monopolistic position of the foreign multinational firm.

Labour-oriented investment was undertaken in labour-intensive industries (such as textiles, shoes, toys) for which home countries had lost comparative advantage, usually due to rising labour costs. Such investment complemented less developed countries which have scarcity of capital but abundant labour. It assisted in the reorganization of the international division of labour and promoted trade between labour-scarce and labour-abundant countries. It increased the import of capital goods from developed to developing countries. And, as this type of investment aimed to establish an export-base rather than import substitution, it increased export of labour-intensive products from developing countries back to the home country or to third countries.

Market-oriented investment in Kojima's scheme was direct investment induced by trade barriers in the host country. Often developing countries imposed differential tariffs, heavier on final consumer goods but lower on intermediate and capital goods. This cascading tariff structure induced foreign firms to import components and parts and assemble them into consumer goods for sale in the domestic market of the host country. This type of investment was trade-creating, but often one-sided. It increased export of components, parts and capital goods from the home to the host country. But since the original purpose of protection was to encourage import-substitution industries, foreign investment induced by this kind of protection rarely led to increased exports of manufactures. It could even be detrimental to the host country if the high degree of protection enabled the firm to produce and sell above the world market price. In the short term the lop-sided trade impact was likely to weigh on the host country's balance of trade. But if the import-substitution industry grew successfully towards export orientation, then direct foreign investment of this type could turn out to be labour-oriented investment and could generate trade from the host country.

Kojima's fourth type of direct investment was labelled "oligopolistic direct foreign investment". It was a variant of the market-oriented type, essentially similar to the direct investment described by Hymer and Vernon with respect to the United States, namely direct investment in products which commanded oligopolistic positions in the market because of product differentiation and other

firm-specific advantages. This type of investment, according to
Kojima, was anti-trade creating in two different ways. First, from
the point of view of the home country, the transfer of production to
a foreign location reduced exports and might eventually increase
imports as products were imported back from the overseas
subsidiary to the home country. In his words, "Both the loss of
foreign markets and increase in imports then result in balance of
payments difficulties and the 'export of job opportunities'" (Kojima
1978, p. 89). Second, from the point of view of the host country, the
demand for inputs (foreign exchange, labour, skill) in the newly
located industries tended to restrict the availability of such inputs
for traditional industries in which the host country had a comparative advantage in world trade. As such it diminished the host
country's capacity for export growth.

Kojima argued that American foreign investment was mainly of
the fourth type. It had occurred mostly in products which involved
high expenditure in R&D and advertising by large firms, and which
as a result commanded highly oligopolistic positions in the market.
By contrast, Kojima contended, Japanese foreign investment
consisted mainly of the first three types.[6] He argued that Japanese
investment in Southeast Asia in the 1960s and 1970s was concentrated in product areas such as textiles, iron and steel, and
agriculture. And he pointed out that these were traditional, price-
competitive goods in which Japan and other developed countries
had been losing their comparative advantage, largely on account of
rising labour costs.[7] Japanese investments were thus complementary to the factor endowments of developing countries, and
tended to encourage trade, promote the international division of
labour, and aid the industrialization of host developing countries.

In Kojima's analysis, foreign investment was usually induced
by changes in comparative advantage within the framework of a
competitive market. Yet he admitted that there could be specific
situations in which foreign investment was induced by imperfections in the market. These imperfections might be created by
the oligopolistic advantages of firms, or by the price distortions of
tariff policies. Yet Kojima placed more emphasis on the framework
of comparative advantage because of its relevance to the bulk of
Japanese overseas investment in the late 1960s and 1970s. His
main contribution to the theory of foreign direct investment was to
focus attention on the international division of labour resulting
from changes in comparative advantage.

In the years following its publication, Kojima's approach was criticized from two angles. First, some economists disagreed with Kojima's view on the determinants of Japanese investment and his emphasis on comparative advantage. Second, others disputed the welfare implications of Kojima's model, particularly his argument that the Japanese style of foreign investment promoted trade, the international division of labour, and complementary development.

Several writers argued that Kojima's sharp distinction between the motivations of Japanese and American investment was misleading. Sekiguchi and Krause pointed out that the Japanese pattern of foreign direct investment in the 1960s and 1970s reflected merely the stages of economic development of Japan and Asian countries at that particular period (Sekiguchi and Krause 1980). As Japan moves up the technological scale and becomes more like the United States, they suggested, Japan would invest more in innovative products, and the pattern of Japanese direct investment would become more like that of the United States. In other words, the distinction which Kojima drew between "Japanese" and "American" motivations for overseas investment was really a distinction between countries in the early and later phases of industrial maturity. And as a result, it was likely to change over time.[8]

In a study comparing American and Japanese direct investment in South Korea, Lee (1984) confirmed this analysis.[9] In the period 1962 to 1972, Japanese investment did tend to be a little more labour-intensive than American. But there was a change in pattern over the next six years, when both American and Japanese direct investment in South Korea became concentrated in skill-intensive, high-technology industries.

Building on this analysis, Lee argued that Kojima had under-estimated the importance of micro-economic factors in his theory of foreign investment. Lee accepted that foreign investment took place within an overall framework of comparative advantage in which resource constraints and government policies (both home and host) played an important role. But Lee added that decisions to invest were taken at the individual firm level. Even when confronted by resource constraints and changes in comparative advantage, Japanese firms faced a range of options. They could switch product lines, concentrate on the home market, or even stop production and convert their capital to stocks. An adequate theory needed to explain why firms would choose to invest overseas. In

Lee's opinion, this theory would need to return to the organization approach of Caves and Vernon.

Several writers suggested that Japanese investment in ASEAN in the 1980s had many similarities to the American style described by the organization theorists, and which Kojima had disavowed. As Japanese firms faced strong competition from the Asian NICs particularly in markets such as consumer electronics, Japanese investment in ASEAN displayed many of the oligopolistic characteristics of American firms. And Japanese firms became as adept as any American multinational at developing brand names and other forms of product differentiation in order to reap oligopolistic advantages.[10]

Several critics have attacked the welfare implications of Kojima's theory. Komoda (1986, p. 10) pointed out that the notion of maximization of global welfare implicit in Kojima's comparative cost model presupposed perfect competition and truly free trade, whereas in fact international trade and investment were characterized by oligopoly. Kojima's picture of "complementarity" between Japanese investment and host country needs (particularly in ASEAN) has been severely attacked. In the 1960s and 1970s a major part of Japanese direct investment in ASEAN went into consumer goods industries supplying the domestic market of host countries. Much of this investment was induced by the import tariffs imposed on consumer goods. This kind of investment encouraged export of machinery, semi-processed raw materials, components and parts from Japan which were used to assemble final consumer goods for the host markets. The investment induced trade, as Kojima predicted, but it was mostly a one-way trade from Japan to ASEAN.[11]

Others have pointed out that Japanese overseas investment has promoted the international division of labour, but often an *intra-firm* international division of labour with limited benefits for host countries.[12] Japanese firms transferred abroad a part of their production system, but tended to use foreign investment to retain close management control. Through techniques such as transfer pricing, firms may be able to limit the financial benefit to host countries. And through restrictive practices they may be able to limit technology transfer and the dissemination of skills.[13]

The development of the Japanese model [14]

Kojima's major book appeared in the same year as Yoshihara's study of *Japanese Investment in Southeast Asia* (1978), and only a year earlier than Ozawa's *Multinationalism, Japanese Style* (1979).

Like Kojima, Ozawa analysed the outflow of Japanese direct investment within a macro-economic framework. However, Ozawa did not follow Kojima in emphasizing the importance of changes in comparative advantage as the motivation for foreign investment. Instead Ozawa went back to classical growth theory and the Ricardo-Hicksian trap of industrial stagnation. According to this theory an industrial economy could not expand indefinitely. Sooner or later it would encounter "irremovable scarcities".[15] In the case of Japan, Ozawa saw a serious shortage of land, and also natural resources (especially energy and mineral resources) as irremovable scarcities which would limit the prospects for industrial expansion. According to Ozawa (1979, p. 67):

> By the end of the 1960s, the Pacific coastal regions of Japan's mainland, known as Tokaido, were cluttered with factories, with continuous urban industrial sprawl obliterating the rural areas that had once existed. An extremely high density of industrial activities ... resulted in aggravating the malignancies of pollution, congestion, and ecological destruction.

Thus Ozawa continued: "It was no coincidence, then, that Japan's overseas investment suddenly grew in 1968 and has been on the rise rapidly since then". According to Ozawa, Japanese firms were compelled by necessity, caused by the resource constraint at home, to extend their subsidiaries overseas through direct investment. This necessity became more compelling as countries which controlled natural resources demonstrated their ability to withhold or limit supplies, as in the Arab oil crisis in 1973. Thus,

> ... it is no longer either economical or safe for Japan to secure resources in the open market. She must seek as much control as possible of hitherto untapped stocks of resources in addition to securing the conventional flows of developed resources. (Ozawa 1979, p. 236)

And on this score Japan was lucky, Ozawa continued, because "Fortunately, there are still plenty of resources left in the world. The developing countries in particular are eager to seek economic and technical assistance for the development of their resources,

and Japan is more than willing to collaborate with the Third
World." Japan could do this through the expansion of its multinational firms with the Japanese Government providing assistance
and financing for major projects. Ozawa thus stressed both the
macro-economic forces driving Japanese firms to invest overseas,
and the purposeful role of government in providing assistance to
firms for the ultimate benefit of securing resources for the national
economy. Ozawa concluded optimistically that the combined force
of macro-economic logic and governmental support would be
sufficient to overcome the resource constraint of the mature
Japanese economy.

Ozawa's theory had a rather limited scope as it was confined to
resource-based investment which constituted only one segment of
the total, and a segment which would decline as a proportion of the
total in the 1980s. However, Ozawa introduced a major new
element into the analysis by combining the macro-economic logic of
international factor endowments with the powerful influence of
raison d'état.

Kunio Yoshihara had written on topics related to Japanese overseas investment since the early 1970s, but he synthesized his views
in a book which appeared in 1978, the same year as Kojima's. Like
Kojima, Yoshihara explained the outflow of Japanese investment
within an overall framework of comparative advantage. However,
unlike Kojima, Yoshihara used a historical approach which demonstrated the changing character of Japanese investment over time.
Yoshihara allowed that imperfections in the market, particularly
those caused by government (both home and host), could have over-
riding importance in specific situations.

Yoshihara explained the development of Japanese investment
from the mid-1960s to the late 1970s in terms of changes in comparative advantage within a historical context. Yoshihara started
from the premise that foreign investment was a corporate decision
undertaken in the pursuit of higher profit. He took it as given that
Japanese firms invested in Southeast Asia because the region
yielded a higher return than investment in Japan (1978, p. 201),
mainly because of " ... the change in comparative advantage for
some industries, labour intensive industries in particular, and the
pursuit of import-substitution policy in some Southeast Asian
countries" (1978, p. 204). Other contributing factors included the
revaluation of the yen after 1970, and various incentives offered by
the Japanese Government.

At the macro level Yoshihara looked at the conditions which made it possible for Japanese firms to adopt foreign investment as a corporate strategy. These factors operated on both the home and host country sides, and can be described as the "push" (home country) and "pull" (host country) factors.[16] He argued that the relative strength of the push and pull factors varied from period to period, and he drew a distinction between the period before 1969 and the period from 1970 to 1978.

In the period up to 1969, the push factors on the Japan side were the need for raw materials, and the need to expand export markets. On the pull side, ASEAN possessed considerable reserves of natural resources which Japan needed, and showed growth in domestic markets, often protected by high tariff barriers. However, the flow of Japanese investment was constrained by the balance of payments situation, which showed a deficit until 1964, and by government policies designed to overcome this problem. According to the 1949 Foreign Exchange and Foreign Trade Control Law, every overseas investment project was subject to government approval. The government permitted and even encouraged investment in resource-oriented industries which helped ensure a cheap and constant supply of natural materials for Japanese industries. Notable among these were Japanese direct investments in the oil and mining industry in Indonesia. But other forms of overseas investment were restrained.

In 1965 Japan's balance of payments passed into surplus and continued to improve at a rapid rate. In response, the government partially lifted the restriction on foreign investment in 1969, and abolished it altogether in 1971. Thereafter Japanese overseas investment increased at an accelerated rate globally.

From 1969 to the late 1970s, there were several "push" factors tending to increase Japanese investment overseas: the availability of funds for investing overseas; the rising cost of land and labour which, in Kojima's terms, led to changes in comparative advantage between Japan and ASEAN countries, and the high cost of pollution controls imposed by Japanese government regulations on some industries.

In ASEAN, Japanese investment flowed mainly into import-substitution industries, pulled by the relatively low cost of labour and land, the availability of natural resources, the inducement of the high tariff walls, plus the prospects of growth in the internal markets. Japanese investment was concentrated in manufacture or assembly of light consumer goods and durables.

Like Ozawa, Yoshihara allowed an important role for government policy in promoting overseas investment. As Japan's balance of payments surplus accumulated, the Japanese Government began to promote direct investment overseas as a way to help Japanese firms secure a production base to produce cheaply for export. The government provided investing firms with low-interest loans and information services, and also used aid and development programmes to improve the infrastructure of host countries as well as to soften any host country's antagonism against Japanese investment.

But Yoshihara went beyond Ozawa in allocating an important role for the *host* governments as well as the home government. Yoshihara stressed that the change in ASEAN governments' attitude to Japan acted as a pull factor. From 1945 to the mid-1960s, ASEAN governments tended to adopt a hostile attitude to Japan but as Japan settled the reparation question and as the governments in ASEAN began to see the benefits to be obtained from foreign investment, this attitude changed to conciliation, with positive effects for investment inflow.

In sum, Yoshihara analysed Japanese overseas investment within a general framework of comparative advantage, but also allowed that government policies at both the home and host ends could have an important influence. Yoshihara also introduced a strong historical dimension into the analysis and took account of the changing demands of both the home and host economies.

Sekiguchi (1983) looked further into the political dimensions of Japanese foreign investment. Implicitly he too accepted the overall framework of comparative advantage, and his approach was generally in line with that of Yoshihara. However, his major contribution was to explore further the importance of the specifically political context.

Sekiguchi argued that ASEAN economies were attractive to Japanese investment for many reasons, including the high and consistent rates of economic growth which provided prospects for market expansion; inexpensive labour; availability of raw materials; close proximity to Japan which minimized transport cost, and protection policies which favoured import-substitution industries. On the Japanese side, high growth rates in the 1970s increased the demand for resources from ASEAN countries and thus led to increases in Japanese overseas investment. While

Japanese economic growth slowed from the average annual rate of 10.5 per cent in the 1960s to 5.2 per cent in the 1970s, and to around 4 per cent in the early 1980s, rising wages and higher costs of location in Japan continued to impel Japanese investment outwards into ASEAN.

Thus, following the spirit of Kojima, Sekiguchi argued that there was a high degree of complementarity between the economy of Japan on one side and those of ASEAN on the other. Japan depended on ASEAN for natural resources and for markets for its goods. ASEAN needed an increasing flow of capital for economic growth because official aid alone was not sufficient. However, Sekiguchi observed, political pressures from the ASEAN side might obstruct the realization of the benefits of this complementarity.

This could occur in many ways. Japanese investment could arouse resentment as a result of the alleged collusion between local political and business élites and Japanese investors. In countries such as Malaysia and Indonesia, the government's ethnic policies, which place priority on equity participation by the indigenous population, might come into conflict with the Japanese firms' criteria of economic efficiency. Many socio-cultural factors might work against ASEAN co-operation with Japanese capital including the memory of Japan's role in World War II; the fact that ASEAN and Japanese élites were more familiar with Western culture and education than with one another; differences in management style, and the resentment that traditional industries feel against Japanese competition.

In sum, while these four writers analysed Japanese investment from varying standpoints and with varying degrees of sophistication, there were some strong similarities running through their theories. Kojima, Yoshihara, Ozawa and Sekiguchi all approached the analysis of Japanese foreign investment within a framework of comparative advantage. All argued, some more strongly than others, that there existed a basic complementarity between the economies of Japan and ASEAN. None of them paid much attention to the specific characteristics of Japanese firms and none invoked the analytic framework of the organization school for more than a passing reference.

Japanese investment has also been a subject of interest and theoretical analysis by economists in the host countries. And they have been drawn to a rather different framework of analysis.

Japanese investment from the host viewpoint

For several prominent economists writing on Japanese investment from the perspective of host countries in ASEAN, the "specific advantages" framework of the Western economists seemed more appropriate than the approach via comparative advantage. In his study of Japanese investment in ASEAN with special reference to Indonesia, Panglaykim (1983) switched the focus away from comparative advantage and back to the specific advantages of individual firms. Panglaykim discussed pull factors on the ASEAN side, including ASEAN's abundant natural resources and labour; strategic location close to Japan,[17] and industrial policies which favoured import-substitution investment. But Panglaykim's main emphasis lay on the advantages of Japanese firms which induced them to invest overseas.

He classified these advantages into seven elements: a cohesive, disciplined and experienced management based on Japanese culture; possession of technology invented in Japan; availability of capital due to the high rate of savings; government support; international network; vertical and horizontal operation, and a sense of national mission. He argued that Japanese firms wanted involvement in equity participation and management of overseas production rather than merely licensing these specific advantages because these allowed them to make greater profits through exploiting their comparative advantages in management organization and other oligopolistic power. In essence, Panglaykim argued that Japanese direct investment in ASEAN could be explained with the same analyses which the industrial organization theorists applied to American multinationals two decades earlier.

In a study of Japanese firms in Thailand, Pornavalai (1989) concluded that the Japanese firms' main advantage over local competitors lay in their control over technology and in their management style. And he went on to describe how Japanese firms actively preserved their control over technology by restricting the ability of local staff to gain access to this technology. This was a theme echoed in studies from other countries. Studies in Singapore showed that compared to other multinationals, Japanese firms kept a closer control over management, financing and technology transfer, were less advanced in recruiting local staff for managerial and professional positions, and had developed fewer backward and forward linkages with local firms.[18] Similar findings surfaced in studies of Japanese direct investment in other ASEAN countries.[19]

Summary and beyond

The micro-economic theories of foreign direct investment of Western organizational economists explained the superiority of multinational firms in terms of their organizational ability, technology and other advantages over local and foreign competitor firms. This superiority induced oligopolistic foreign direct investment and gave foreign investment a dominant role in industries which required a high level of technology.

Kojima argued that this view of foreign investment had given rise to much resentment against all types of foreign investment in developing countries. It led to a view that foreign investment by multinationals was a necessary evil: necessary because the multinationals possessed the technology which developing countries lack; evil because their main motivation was profitability, based on oligopolistic or monopolistic control of the market. The decision to invest overseas was made in the context of the growth of the firm and had nothing to do with the welfare of recipient countries. What was good for the firm might be undesirable for the recipient countries.

By emphasizing the macro aspect of foreign investment and by arguing that Japanese investment was motivated mainly by changes in comparative advantage based on differences in factor endowment or relative factor costs between Japan and developing countries, Kojima could portray Japanese foreign investment as beneficial to both donor and recipient countries. In his view, foreign investment triggered by changes in comparative advantage in a competitive situation encouraged trade, and helped overcome the recipient countries' lack of capital and know-how. In this way it could contribute to the upgrading of capital, technical know-how, and to the process of industrialization of developing countries via the development of the international division of labour.

Several other Japanese writers emphasized the role changes in comparative advantage played in the determination of Japanese overseas investment. Yoshihara explained Japanese overseas investment in terms of changes in comparative advantage and added greater precision in the definition of the push and pull factors which regulated the flow of overseas investment. As Yoshihara's later work showed, he was much less optimistic than Kojima on the impact on ASEAN industrialization. Indeed Yoshihara (1988) came close to the neo-imperialist theorists in arguing that the lop-sided relationship of Japan and ASEAN tended to reinforce the dependence of ASEAN and to diminish the opportunity for true indigenous industrial development. Ozawa stressed the natural resource constraint of the mature Japanese economy as the main determinant driving foreign investment overseas, and also allocated a strongly positive role for government. In Ozawa's view, Japanese firms would have limited capacity to invest overseas had it not been for government assistance. Sekiguchi argued that complementarity of Japan and ASEAN induced Japanese investment, and analysed the political and cultural factors which could inhibit the full flow.

All of the Japanese writers discussed here would allow that imperfections in the market caused either by government policies such as tariff barriers or by oligopolistic power of individual firms could create situations in which firms would invest overseas to grab or defend markets irrespective of macro considerations of comparative advantage. However, Kojima and Ozawa explicitly argued that this was not the characteristic motivation of Japanese overseas investment, and Yoshihara appeared to assume it was rare. Yet several economists writing from the standpoint of host countries in ASEAN have found an oligopolistic situation dominated by Japanese firms with specific oligopolistic advantages.

All of these approaches shared one important characteristic in common. They all focused their main attention on the supply side of foreign investment. The demand side got scant attention.

For the organization theorists, the motivation of overseas investment arose from the technological advantage, organizational advantage, and oligopolistic environment faced by the investor firm. For Kojima and Yoshihara, the motivation arose from changes in factor endowment, cost structure and government policy in Japan. Factors on the side of the recipient country played an essentially passive role in these theories. In both the Western and Japanese approaches, the availability of factors of production, access to markets, and host government policies had an important bearing on the flow of investment. Yet the role played by these factors in the analysis was that of an influence on the cost of investing overseas. There was no attempt to construct a full theory of the *demand* for foreign investment on the host side to match the theory of supply. In this book, this framework of analysis is extended to include also the demand for foreign investment in the host country. Instead of viewing the recipient countries as having a passive role, the ASEAN countries which play host to Japanese investment are regarded as playing a rather active role in the relationship.

The factors that determine the demand for foreign investment go beyond the issues of investment climate, political stability, popular attitudes and government policy-making. The key factors are the nature and development of capital in the host country.[20]

Briefly, in considering the determinants of the demand for foreign investment, we have to look at what local entrepreneurs (domestic capital) and local governments want out of foreign investment. In this respect, the development of domestic and state capital, their interaction and their relationship with foreign capital are the key factors.

Schematically, it may be postulated that demand for foreign investment is a function of several variables. Firstly, there is the satisfaction or utilities the governments of host countries can obtain from foreign investment inflow. These include contributions to the balance of payments (net increase in capital inflow and exports), employment generation, the rate of growth, upgrading of the technological levels of workers and of different economic sectors. Then there are also contributions which are political in character. Foreign investment may be attractive because it can be regulated more easily than domestic private investment, or because it can be exploited to strengthen state capital vis-à-vis the private sector. Foreign investment could play a role in policies designed to strengthen one particular group. On the other side of the coin, foreign investment may be perceived as a threat to state capital, or as a potential focus of political tension, or as a distorting influence in domestic factor markets.

The second important set of variables are the utilities to be derived from foreign investment by local entrepreneurs or domestic capital. To domestic entrepreneurs, the utilities of foreign investment lie in the profits to be made through joint venture, in the contributions towards the upgrading of technology and marketing and managerial know-how, entrepreneurial skills, and access to external markets. On the negative side, foreign investment may mean increased competition in the same product markets, and competition for scarce resources of infrastructure and manpower.

The host country's demand for foreign investment has direct bearing on the motivation of the foreign investor. If the host country has a high demand for foreign investment, it can reduce the costs and raise the profitability for the incoming firm in various ways. It may reduce costs involved in bureaucratic procedure, in the process of finding partners and suppliers, and in gaining access to infrastructure and information sources; such cost reductions may affect the host country's comparative advantage as an investment site. They work to reduce the transaction costs incurred by foreign investors.

The attitude and bargaining power of domestic capital can also influence the forms which foreign investment takes. If domestic capital wishes to minimize foreign equity control and minimize the foreign exchange costs of acquiring new technology, it may try to restrict traditional forms of direct foreign investment (which involve control or joint control by foreign partners in the running of the enterprise) and force foreign concerns into the new forms of investment such as technology contracts, management contracts and franchise arrangements or licensing agreements (Chee 1988). The new forms of investment may not require direct equity participation which often comes with "some control" by foreign investors, although it may mean a swapping of technology or other agreements for a minority equity share in the enterprise or other arrangements for the returns on the services rendered. In the new forms of investment, foreign investors may have no control in the running of the enterprise. These new forms of investment are increasingly in demand from host country entrepreneurs who wish to have complete control over the various aspects of the enterprise, but who need co-operation from foreign firms for technological and marketing reasons. This demand in turn influences the new direction of foreign participation by foreign investors.[21]

By taking into account the demand factor the host country is considered an active partner in the foreign investment relationship, with influence over both the size of the flow and the forms of the investment. In other words, a theory of foreign investment should analyse the demand side, going beyond the "investment climate" or "political stability" to encompass the interrelationship between state, domestic private and foreign capital in the host country. This approach will be used to analyse the new wave of Japanese investment in ASEAN after 1985.

Notes

1. The gist of the idea about specific advantages of foreign firms is found in the writings of Southard (1931) and Dunning (1958). It was Hymer, in his Ph.D. thesis in 1960 (published 1976), who explored it in depth. For a comprehensive review of early theories, see Dunning (1973), and Hufbauer (1975).
2. It has been pointed out that while the product cycle approach starts out in the world of organization theory, it ends up in the world of comparative advantage. In the final stage, it is the lower cost of labour or the changes in comparative advantage between developed and developing countries based on differences in factor endowment which are introduced to explain foreign investment in developing countries. See Kojima (1978) and Yoshihara (1978).
3. This approach follows the transaction costs analyses of Coase (1937) and Williamson (1973) to explain why the ability to internalize economic activities to minimize transaction costs makes a firm prefer direct foreign investment in developing countries. See Kojima (1978) and Yoshihara (1978).
4. See also Casson (1983, 1987), and Dunning (1981).
5. Foreign investment appears to have become a major topic of interest for Japanese economists following the Tanaka tour and the outburst of criticism against Japanese activity in ASEAN in the mid-1970s. See for instance the collection of seminar papers in Mori (1976). The major works of Kojima, Yoshihara and Ozawa all appeared in the two years 1978–79.
6. Sekiguchi and Krause (1980), while not rejecting the Kojima hypothesis, disagreed with his normative conclusions. They argued that Kojima may have exaggerated the welfare benefits of Japanese direct investment and underestimated the welfare gain of American investment. They maintained that American-type investment could also be beneficial to developing countries as "American style investment with its new technology and advanced management may make a unique and significant contribution to the welfare of a host country with spread effects throughout the economy". See Sekiguchi and Krause (1980), pp. 438–39. On this normative aspect see further discussion in Sekiguchi and Krause (1980), pp. 447–52).
7. It is worth pointing out that Kojima's argument concentrates on changes in comparative advantage induced by changes in comparative labour costs, but could be generalized to incorporate other kinds of shifts. For instance, the increased cost of pollution control in Japan due to more stringent government policies raises the relative cost of production in Japan and this in itself will increase the comparative advantage of developing countries where pollution controls are more slack. The increase in land prices and other factors' costs in Japan

relative to other developing countries also leads to changes in comparative advantage. So too do shifts in currency exchange rates.

8. Arndt (1974) observed that Kojima had not really constructed a comprehensive theory of foreign investment, but had merely drawn attention to the divergence between the the private interest of foreign investors and the public interest. Lee (1984) argued that Kojima failed to establish a plausible micro-economic basis for his macro-economic theory of direct foreign investment.

9. See also Heimenz (1987) who compared the pattern of West German, Japanese and American investment in ASEAN manufacturing. Heimenz concluded that while differences may be observed in the patterns of investment by different countries, over time they have converged. Heimenz argues this is because, over time, the technology differences between the three investing countries have become less marked.

10. Indeed it could be argued that there is nothing unique in the Japanese pattern. Kojima's thesis is now most relevant to the NICs, since they are replicating Japan's pattern ten to fifteen years earlier. The author would like to thank Hal Hill for suggesting this point.

11. See Seiji Naya and Narongchai Akrasanee (1974), Allen (1973a), Thee (1984), and Hill (1988).

12. See for example Tran Van Tho (1987).

13. Kojima argued that foreign investment induced by changes in comparative advantage led to fuller use of surplus resources of developing host countries in Southeast Asia. The experience of Singapore may indeed support his argument. During the 1960s and 1970s, the government encouraged foreign investment of all nationalities in labour-intensive, export-oriented products in order to reduce unemployment and quicken the process of industrialization. See Lim Chong Yah and Associates (1988). The government pursued a free trade regime and much of the success must be attributed to foreign investment promotion in a free trade situation. But foreign investment in Singapore did not take place within the context of a completely laissez-faire economy. The Singapore government's industrial promotion and skills training policies had much to do with the success.

14. In this review we focus on the writings by four major Japanese scholars in the period after 1974. But an earlier work in English by Thomas W. Allen deserves a mention. In his 1973 study of direct investment by Japanese enterprises in Southeast Asia, Allen looked at the general motives of Japanese firms, and at the ways import-substitution policies encouraged Japanese investment in assembly ventures. From his survey, Allen concluded that Japanese firms made little profit from assembly operations but did make substantial profits in trade in parts and components manufactured in Japan, and from royalty payments

negotiated as part of joint-venture arrangements with local firms. Allen also concluded that Japanese firms were focusing on long-term advantages to be gained from establishing a significant position in host-country markets. Allen's conclusions are generally in line with those of the organization school of Western economists. Japanese firms were generally motivated to invest overseas in order to leverage their specific advantages through such devices as royalty arrangements, and in order to gain oligopolistic power in expanding host-country markets.

15. A term used by J.R. Hicks, cited in Ozawa (1979), p. 65.

16. Yoshihara did not use the "push" and "pull" terminology, but it offers a convenient way to summarize his argument.

17. On this same point, Hill emphasizes "... the key role Indonesia occupied in Japan's commercial and strategic policies towards the region. Indonesia was — and is — the dominant power in ASEAN, in Japan's view, and the strong economic complementarity between the two countries — particularly in the resource trade — reinforced Japan's interest. Consequently, a range of measures (aid, trade and political initiatives) spurred Japanese investments ...". See Hill (1988), p. 72.

18. See for example Chng et al. (1986).

19. Chinwanno and Tambunlertchai (1983), Chng and Hirono (1984), Chee and Lee (1983), Dorodjatun Kuntjoro-Jakti (1983), Hill (1988, pp. 63–70), Komoda (1986), Nathabhol et al. (1987), Ng et al. (1986), and Santikarn (1981), Thee (1984a), United Nations (1987).

20. While labour's view could also be important, labour unions in ASEAN are still weak and it will be some time before labour groups will be mature enough to be able to influence foreign investment policies.

21. The term foreign participation is used here (other writers have called it overseas activity or intermediate forms of overseas activity) as some of the new forms of investment may not be categorized as "investment" because they do not involve a flow of equity from home to host country. Indeed, in a case where a technology contract is swapped for a small equity share, there may not be any effect on the balance of payments. In this sense, the recorded figures of direct foreign investment will always understate the true extent of foreign participation in a host country, although the returns in terms of remittances going out will be recorded. See further details on the different types of the new forms of investment by Japanese firms in Nakakita (1988).

3

The Japanese origins of the new wave

The major works on Japanese overseas investment all appeared in the mid- and late 1970s and inevitably they reflected the specific conditions of that time. Japanese investment of that period was concentrated in resource extraction, in import-substitution manufacture for the host market, and in the production of parts and components required by final manufacturers in Japan. Within Asia, the majority of Japanese investment projects were in the newly industrializing countries (NICs).

In the decade since these major works appeared, the nature of Japanese overseas investment has changed dramatically, both in scale and character. Now export-oriented projects dominate. And within Asia, ASEAN has assumed greater importance. Most of this change has been concentrated in the past five years.

This chapter examines the new wave of Japanese investment, its motivations from the supply side, and the key characteristics of its impact on ASEAN. It begins with an explanation of what the new wave is by briefly reviewing the main characteristics of the old wave of Japanese investment from the 1960s to the mid-1980s, and then presents the key facts concerning the scale and features of Japanese investment in the region since 1984. Next, the chapter examines the processes driving Japanese capital to flow overseas on this new scale. This involves an extended discussion of structural change in the Japanese economy as background for understanding the roles of trade friction and the yen appreciation in driving Japanese capital to venture overseas. Finally the chapter examines key characteristics of new-wave Japanese ventures in ASEAN, in particular their choice of location, the establishment of networks of linked firms across ASEAN, their increased use of local content, and the changing character of the overseas investing Japanese firm.

This chapter aims to show how much the new wave of investment differs from that described in the "classic" works on Japanese overseas investment by Kojima, Yoshihara and Ozawa. The theoretical and practical implications of these differences are held over until Chapter 5.

Japanese investment in ASEAN before 1985: The old wave[1]

The flow of investment out of Japan and into Asia increased steadily from the mid-1950s onwards. In the period up to 1985 (the old wave), three major trends can be identified. First, Japanese investment sought to secure supplies of raw materials which were scarce in Japan. Second, Japanese firms relocated manufacturing processes to countries with lower production costs. Third, Japanese firms established subsidiaries in countries which had erected tariff barriers to encourage import substitution.

The relocation of manufacturing processes occurred largely in labour-intensive industries in which Japan was losing comparative advantage. The first major industry to be affected was textiles, and many textile firms relocated in the early 1970s. In 1973, for instance, 39 per cent of all Japanese direct investment in Asia went into textiles. In the late 1970s, the focus switched to steel, non-ferrous metals and chemicals. After 1980 it switched again to transport equipment and electrical machinery (Tran Van Tho 1987).

The favoured sites for relocation were the Asian NICs, especially Taiwan, Korea, and Hong Kong. In the 1960s, two-thirds of all projects (by number) in Asia were in this sub-region. In the 1970s the proportion declined to around half, and declined further to about a quarter in the early 1980s. Many of the firms relocating to these new sites were not final producers, but subcontractors manufacturing parts and components which required labour-intensive processes. Some were small and medium scale enterprises producing for export to third countries.

Within ASEAN, Japanese investment was concentrated in resource extraction. By 1985, 48 per cent of the total stock of Japanese investment in ASEAN was concentrated in resource-related projects, especially in Indonesia. Between 1973 and 1985, Indonesia was the main destination for Japanese investment within ASEAN in every year except one (1979). In this period, only the United States received a greater share of Japanese investment than Indonesia (Chee 1989b).

Japanese capital began investing in import-substitution projects in ASEAN in the 1960s. This form of investment increased through the 1970s, and then tailed off. In the early 1970s, Philippines was a favourite destination, but investment there subsequently declined and more flowed to Malaysia and Thailand.

Japanese export-oriented investment first came to Singapore in the mid-1960s, focusing on shipbuilding and repair, watchmaking, toys, electrical machinery, and electrical parts and components. Later, this type of investment also flowed to Malaysia, but only to a limited extent, and before 1985 it was virtually insignificant in the other ASEAN countries (Yoshihara 1978).

The United States continued to be the largest foreign investor in Indonesia, Singapore and Thailand until the late 1970s, but from then onwards Japan played that role in every ASEAN state.

As a proportion of the total *number* of Japanese investment projects in Asia, ASEAN had a relatively insignificant share. In the 1960s, only 10 per cent of all the Japanese projects in Asia were in ASEAN. The figure rose to around 16 per cent in the late 1960s but subsequently fell back to around 10–12 per cent.[2] However, the average size of projects located in ASEAN was relatively large compared to the small and medium scale subcontractor projects which characterized Japanese investment in the Asian NICs. Thus by 1985 the total stock of Japanese investment in ASEAN exceeded that in the NICs by around two-and-a-half times: US$12.5 billion versus US$5.4 billion (Chee 1989b).

Japanese investment projects in ASEAN tended to be carried out by major Japanese conglomerates. Sumitomo, Mitsubishi, Toyota, Nissan, Honda, Minebea, Sharp, Matsushita, Sony and Toshiba all had ventures in the region. Also, these projects were generally joint ventures rather than fully-owned subsidiaries. In many cases these joint-venture projects developed·from principal-distributor relationships when host government regulations raised tariff barriers and stipulated local majority shareholdings for assembly and manufacturing projects (Panglaykim 1983; Pornavalai 1989).[3]

In sum, Japanese investment in ASEAN before 1985 was concentrated in resource extraction, especially in Indonesia, and to a lesser extent in import-substitution manufacture. Most of the manufacturing projects were joint ventures between a Japanese conglomerate and a local partner. In this period, export-oriented investment had favoured the NICs more than ASEAN because of their more mature industrial base and because of the export orientation of their development policies. Some export-oriented investment had flowed to Singapore and to a lesser extent Malaysia, but elsewhere in ASEAN it was insignificant.

The scale of the new wave

Japanese investment in ASEAN after 1985 constitutes a new wave because of a change in both scale and character.

In the 1970s and early 1980s, the flow of Japanese investment into ASEAN averaged around US$400 million per annum. In 1984 this rose to US$906 million, and then jumped again to US$1,524 million in 1987 (Table 3.1).[4] At the same time, ASEAN's share of total world-wide foreign investment actually declined as a result of the very large increase in flows to the United States. However, for ASEAN it was the absolute amount rather than the share which counted. There was also a marked shift in the character of Japanese investment coming to ASEAN. Export-oriented projects figured to an extent unprecedented in earlier years.[5]

Moreover, these shifts in scale and character changed the overall significance of Japanese investment for the economies of the ASEAN region. The relative size of Japanese investment in total domestic private investment in each of the ASEAN countries is not that significant.[6] However, the impact on the process of industrialization will be much more substantial than the simple proportions suggest. MITI (Japan's Ministry of Trade and Industry) forecasts that the volume of goods produced overseas by Japanese firms will rise from 4.2 per cent of Japanese Gross Domestic

Table 3.1

Japan's foreign direct investment on a country basis
(In US$ millions and percentages)

	FY 1951–83 Accumulated amount		FY 1984ᵃ		FY 1985		FY 1986		FY 1987	
Korea	1,471	(2.4)ᵇ	107	(1.1)	134	(1.1)	436	(2.0)	647	(1.9)
Taiwan	581	(0.9)	65	(0.6)	114	(0.9)	291	(1.3)	367	(1.1)
Hong Kong	2,388	(3.9)	412	(4.1)	131	(1.1)	502	(2.3)	1,072	(3.2)
Singapore	1,705	(2.8)	225	(2.2)	339	(2.8)	302	(1.4)	494	(1.5)
Indonesia	7,641	(12.5)	374	(3.7)	408	(3.3)	250	(1.1)	545	(1.6)
Malaysia	904	(1.5)	142	(1.4)	79	(0.6)	158	(0.7)	163	(0.5)
Philippines	785	(1.3)	46	(0.5)	61	(0.5)	21	(0.1)	72	(0.2)
Thailand	593	(1.0)	119	(1.2)	48	(0.4)	124	(0.6)	250	(0.7)
ASEAN	11,628	(19.0)	906	(8.9)	935	(7.6)	855	(3.8)	1,524	(4.6)
China	73	(0.1)	114	(1.1)	100	(0.8)	226	(1.0)	1,226	(3.7)
Oceania	3,271	(5.3)	120	(1.2)	491	(4.0)	974	(4.4)	1,343	(4.0)
USA	16,536	(27.0)	3,359	(33.1)	5,395	(44.2)	10,165	(45.5)	14,704	(44.1)
Europe	7,135	(11.6)	1,937	(19.1)	1,930	(15.8)	3,469	(15.5)	6,576	(19.7)
World total	61,278	(100.0)	10,155	(100.0)	12,217	(100.0)	22,320	(100.0)	33,364	(100.0)

a FY = Fiscal year ending 31 March of the next year.
b Figures in parentheses show world share in percentages.
SOURCE: Ministry of Finance as reported in Nakakita (1988), p. 308.

Product (GDP) in 1984 to 8.3 per cent by 1993, and that between a third and a quarter of the increase will be located in Asia. That means overseas production by Japanese firms will rise from around US$52 billion in 1984 to S$380 billion in 1993, and that approximately US$57 to US$75 billion of the increase will be located in Asia.[7] This figure is more than the total industrial output of ASEAN today. Of course not all of this Asian total will be located in ASEAN, but it is conceivable that ASEAN will receive a major portion. Japanese investment looks set to play a major role in a new phase of export-oriented industrialization in ASEAN.

Explaining the new wave

The spurt in Japanese overseas investment after 1985 is often explained solely in terms of the yen appreciation.[8] The argument runs as follows. The appreciation of the yen made Japanese products less attractive in terms of price in international markets. Faced with the prospect of declining sales, Japanese firms were obliged to relocate production to countries which had lower manufacturing costs and rates of exchange that were unlikely to appreciate *vis-à-vis* Japan's major trading partners in the near future.

A second popular explanation focuses on trade friction with the United States and the European Community. According to this argument, Japan's trade surplus prompted its major trading partners to impose tariffs, quotas or non-trade barriers against Japanese exports. To overcome this trade friction, Japanese firms started to invest in those deficit countries to promote growth, employment and a better trade balance, and to circumvent the trade barriers. Some firms invested in ASEAN countries in order to make use of these countries' unfilled Generalized System of Preferences (GSP) quotas, thereby getting around the trade barriers in the United States and the European Community.

There is no doubt that the steep yen appreciation between 1985 and 1986 accelerated the need of Japanese firms to invest overseas. But the real forces behind both the yen appreciation and the relocation overseas are much more fundamental and had been operating in the Japanese economy for some time. They are embedded in the transformation of Japan from an industrial country relying on labour-intensive exports into a high-tech economy. It is argued here that structural change within the Japanese economy was the fundamental cause pushing a large flow of foreign investment out from Japan. The yen appreciation and trade frictions were symptoms of this transformation.

The transformation of the Japanese economy[9]

In the 1950s and 1960s, Japan experienced rapid growth of around 10 per cent per annum. This rate of growth was triggered initially by the procurement boom associated with the Korean War and later by the similar procurement boom associated with the Vietnam War between 1965 and 1972. Expansion in domestic demand added to this impetus. In the 1970s, growth slowed to 6.1 per cent, and in 1980–87 slowed further to 3.7 per cent (MITI 1988a). The deceleration after 1970 can be explained to some extent by the adverse effects of the first and second oil price increases and the impact of the world recession. But it has also been argued that the principal factor causing the economic slow-down was the sharp decline in the rate of growth of domestic investment in the 1970s and especially after 1979. This was largely the outcome of two government policies, wage restraint and austere fiscal management, which generally dampened enthusiasm for increased domestic investment.

However, after 1974, the decline in domestic investment was offset by a remarkable surge in productivity due to increased Research and Development (R&D), greater use of robots and improved management. Productivity in manufacturing grew at the high rate of 9.2 per cent per annum between 1975 and 1979. In addition, the slowing down in domestic demand was compensated by a rapid growth of exports at an average rate of around 18 per cent per annum in nominal terms in the period 1973–79 (Thorn 1988, p. 4). Thus despite the recession in the 1980s, Japan's economic growth was still quite high compared to other developed countries. By the beginning of the 1980s, four significant changes had occurred in the Japanese economy: first, a shift in the sectoral structure; second, changes in labour conditions; third, dramatic changes within the industrial sector; and finally a rise in exports.

Sectoral structure

Up to 1970, the most rapidly growing sector of the Japanese economy was the secondary sector, especially manufacturing. Yet after 1970, the share of manufacturing in Japanese GDP remained more or less constant around 30 per cent, while the total contribution of the secondary sector actually declined. Meanwhile, the tertiary sector took over as the main engine of growth. Its share of GDP expanded from 46.4 per cent in 1970 to 55.9 per cent in 1985 (Table 3.2).

There was a parallel shift in the pattern of employment. In the mid-1950s, the primary sector still employed nearly 40 per cent of Japan's total labour force. By 1985, its share had been reduced to 9 per cent. The labour share in the secondary sector increased from 29 per cent in 1950 to 42 per cent in 1970, and then remained more or less constant at around 34 to 35 per cent. Meanwhile, the tertiary sector continued to expand until 1985 when it absorbed 57 per cent of the total employed labour force.

Within the tertiary sector the most dynamic subsectors were electronics, telecommunications, and information technology. By 1984, total employment in these subsectors amounted to 1.6 million persons (Imai 1988). The development of high technology and the information industry is expected to spearhead the economic growth of Japan in the future.

Labour conditions

Throughout the period of rapid economic growth, the unemployment rate was low — around 2 to 3 per cent — and even during the recession in the early 1980s, the unemployment rate remained at the same level (Japan Economic Research Centre 1988). As the normal labour supply (full-time workers) became fully occupied, firms drew in more and more casual and temporary workers, many of whom were housewives. In the 1980s, tight conditions in the labour markets, especially for unskilled and semi-skilled workers, led to increasing use of illegal migrant workers from developing countries, mainly in construction and small-scale enterprises.[10]

In such tight labour market conditions, labour costs should soar. Yet between 1975 and 1985 the government was able to impose a wage restraint policy and restrict the rise in real wages to a rate well below the rate of increase of productivity. Government won

Table 3.2
Structure of Japan's GNP and employment 1955–1985
(In percentages)

GNP[a] and employment	1955	1960	1965	1970	1975	1980	1985	1992
GNP (¥ billion)	7,299.0	15,487.0	32,657.0	73,128.0	147,874.0	235,834.0	321,513.0	436,000.0[b]
Primary	22.7	14.6	11.2	7.4	5.5	3.5	3.2	1.6
Secondary	37.8	45.7	44.4	46.5	42.4	41.7	40.9	35.5
Manufacturing	22.7	29.3	27.9	30.4	30.7	29.5	30.2	28.2
Tertiary	39.2	39.9	44.7	46.4	52.1	54.8	55.9	62.9
Employment (thousand)	40,900.0	44,360.0	47,300.0	50,940.0	52,230.0	55,360.0	58,170.0	61,370.0
Primary	37.6	30.2	23.5	17.4	12.5	10.3	8.7	7.1
Secondary	29.1	33.4	38.1	42.1	35.2	34.7	34.3	32.0
Manufacturing	24.4	28.0	31.9	35.2	25.7	24.7	25.0	22.9
Tertiary	33.4	36.4	38.4	40.4	52.3	55.0	57.0	50.9

a All GNP figures are in nominal terms.
b For 1993.

SOURCE: Economic Planning Agency, *National Income Statistics*; and Bureau of Statistics, *Labour Force Surveys*; Japan Economic Research Centre, *Five-Year Economic Forecast FY 1988–92* (Tokyo, February 1988).

support for the policy on the grounds that the two oil price rises threatened to force up prices and undermine Japan's competitiveness in world markets. However, in the mid-1980s, the rise in the yen made oil cheap and destroyed this rationale. Wages began to rise and, more importantly, are expected to rise higher in the future. Compared to other industrial powers, Japanese wage costs are still below average. But this situation is not expected to last much longer.

Industrial restructuring

In the early 1970s, heavy industries began to face difficulties because of high energy and raw material costs, and increased competition from Asian NICs. Yet Japan maintained her competitiveness in world markets by inventing energy-saving devices and by developing new products through larger investments in R&D, both on the part of government and individual firms.

In the 1970s, precision machinery, automobile and transport machinery (with the exception of ships) figured among the ranks of rapidly growing industries. Following the first and especially the second oil price crises, industries such as steel, chemicals and non-ferrous metals, dependent on high-cost raw materials and oil, began to face difficulties due to increasing competition from Korea and other countries.

However, through rationalization, energy conservation and stringent management practices, Japan began to shift the industrial structure away from heavy industry and chemicals towards sophisticated electronics, information technology, machine production and entertainment goods. In the period 1975–83, electrical machinery contributed over a fifth of the total growth in Japanese manufacturing output. In the period 1980–83, this subsector's contribution increased to over two-fifths. By the early 1980s, Japan's most rapidly growing export products were mostly from the electronics subsector: video recorders and tapes, NC machines, industrial robots, integrated circuits, computers and office automation equipment (Ng, Hirono and Akrasanee 1987, p. 57).

The rise in exports

In the 1970s Japan's major export markets were in Asia. The expanding Asian economies, especially in East and Southeast Asia,

were the main markets for much of Japanese consumer, intermediate and capital goods. In the 1980s, the export market in Asia
expanded at a slower rate, and domestic demand also slackened.
Japan increasingly became dependent on exports to the United
States and Europe. The United States in particular became Japan's
largest market, absorbing as much as 36.5 per cent of Japan's total
exports. The next largest markets were Korea and Germany, which
absorbed much lower proportions of Japan's exports — 5.8 and 5.6
per cent — respectively (MITI 1988a).

From 1981 onwards, Japan showed a surplus on its current
account. Between 1984 and 1988, these surpluses ran at a level of 3
to 5 per cent of Gross National Product (GNP) (Table 3.3). Japan's
success in maintaining relatively high export growth in the 1980s
was due to several factors: general government support including
the wage restraint policy;[11] the ability of Japanese firms to reduce
all-round costs in order to offset rising energy costs in the early
1980s; the ability to raise labour productivity; success in maintaining inflation at 2 to 3 per cent per annum through tight fiscal
policies, and finally the undervaluation of the yen. In contrast, the
United States responded to the oil-price rise by boosting the value
of the dollar (thereby abetting the low yen strategy) in order to
avoid having to cut the budget deficit or to increase taxes.

In sum, Japan had been transformed from a low-wage economy
concentrated in heavy industry, to an economy focused on high-
technology industries and services with rapidly rising wage rates.
Japan had effected this transformation by exploiting export
markets in the developed world. When she then reacted to the oil
price rise by upgrading productivity and depressing the currency,
Japan became the world's most competitive exporter and soon
developed a massive trade surplus. When this surplus then
triggered a revaluation of the currency, Japanese firms needed to
adopt new methods to exploit their advances in high technology
and high productivity. They had to stop treating the world as
simply their market place, and start treating it as their production
platform as well.

The yen appreciation

By 1985 Japan had accumulated an enormous surplus in the
balance of trade and current account, while most of her major

Table 3.3
Japan's balance of trade
(*In US$ billions*)

	1975	1980	1982	1983	1984	1985	1986	1987[a]	1988[a]	1992[a]
Exports	56.0	134.9	136.0	150.7	167.9	180.7	211.3	229.7	249.3	287.7
Imports	50.2	128.2	115.9	116.2	122.3	119.1	109.6	136.0	153.2	219.7
Balance of trade	5.8	6.7	20.1	34.5	45.6	61.6	101.6	93.7	96.1	6.8
Balance of current account	1.0	-7.0	9.1	24.2	37.0	55.0	94.1	84.1	87.7	73.5
	(0.0)[b]	(-0.6)	(0.8)	(2.0)	(3.0)	(3.8)	(4.5)	(3.4)	(3.1)	(1.8)

a Forecasts.
b Figures in parenthesis are balance of current accounts as percentages of GNP.
SOURCE: The Bank of Japan, *Balance of Payments Monthly*. Forecast figures from 1987–92, Japan Economic Research Centre, *Five-Year Economic Forecast FY 1988–92*.

trading partners had to contend with a huge trade deficit, especially the United States (US$117.7 billion in 1985, US$141.4 billion in 1986). The imbalances in trade between Japan and the major developed countries gave rise to heightened trade friction especially between Japan on the one hand and the United States and Europe on the other. By 1985 it was felt that the absurd yen/dollar ratio posed a serious threat to global financial stability. Thus the meeting of the Group of Five (G5) in August 1985 to formulate policies to allow the dollar to fall.

After this meeting, direct government intervention in the foreign exchange markets combined with interest rate manipulations by central banks led to a dramatic devaluation of the dollar, especially against the yen (Table 3.4). The yen had been appreciating gradually against the dollar for many years. In the fourteen years from 1971 to 1984, the yen had risen 47 per cent against the dollar. But the rise after 1985 was unprecedentedly steep and dramatic. In two-and-a-half years from 31 August 1985 to 28 April 1988, the yen value in terms of the dollar appreciated by 89 per cent.

The impact on export industries[12]

While the yen had been appreciating gradually between 1970 and 1984, Japanese exporters had largely managed to remain competitive by improving productivity. The sharp yen appreciation after 1985 however changed the picture very suddenly. Prices of Japanese exports in the world market soared, and the volume of exports started to decline. For example the volume of automobile export declined 4.5 per cent in 1987.

The yen appreciation exacerbated Japan's problems in competing against a new set of players in the market for modern consumer durables: the four Asian NICs of Korea, Taiwan, Hong Kong and Singapore. In recent years they had emerged as efficient producers of consumer electronics and, in the case of Korea, of automobiles and some industrial electronics.

One way to measure the relative position of a country for a certain product is to calculate the RCA (or revealed comparative advantage) index, which is $(E^i/E_h)/W^i/W$, where E^i is export of product^i by country$_h$, E_h is total exports of the country, W^i is the world total export of product^i, and W is world total exports. If the ratio is greater than one this means the country is enjoying some

Table 3.4
Changes of value of selected currencies
(US$ per national currency)[a]

	Japan Yen	Indonesia Rupiahs	Malaysia Dollar	Singapore Dollar	Thailand Baht	South Korea Won	Hong Kong[b] Dollar		Taiwan[b] NT$
1971	349.8	393.4	3.05	3.05	20.8	350.8			
1976	296.6	415.0	2.54	2.47	20.4	484.0	4.8	(3 Aug)	37.9
1980	226.7	627.0	2.18	2.14	20.5	607.4	4.9	(20 Aug)	36.0
1981	220.5	631.8	2.30	2.11	21.8	681.0	5.9	(20 Aug)	36.3
1982	249.1	661.4	2.33	2.14	23.0	731.1	4.0	(23 Aug)	39.0
1983	237.5	909.3	2.32	2.11	23.0	775.8	7.4	(15 Aug)	40.0
1984	237.5	1,025.9	2.34	2.11	23.7	806.0	7.8	(8 Aug)	39.0
31 Aug 1985	236.9								
1985	238.5	1,110.6	2.48	2.20	27.2	870.0	7.7	(19 Aug)	39.2
1986	168.5	1,282.6	2.58	2.18	26.3	881.4	7.8	(4 Aug)	37.8
1987	144.6	1,643.8	2.52	2.11	25.7	822.6	7.8	(1 Aug)	30.1
28 Apr 1988	125.3								
Aug 1988	133.6	1,696.5	2.65	2.04	25.5	722.8	7.8	(1 Aug)	28.6
Jan–Aug 1988	128.4	1,672.6	2.59	2.02	25.3	746.2			

a Unless otherwise stated the rates are average market rate for the period.
b Spot rate on the date specified.

SOURCE: Hong Kong and Taiwan: *Far Eastern Economic Review*, various issues. For other countries: IMF *International Financial Statistics*, various years.

comparative advantage. The higher the ratio, the greater the comparative advantage the country has in relation to other countries in the export of the product.

Figure 3.1 shows RCA changes by major industrial groups in Japan, the four NICs (Hong Kong, Korea, Singapore, Taiwan), and the remaining ASEAN states (Indonesia, Malaysia, Philippines and Thailand) in the period 1970–79.[13] The data show that by 1979, Japan no longer had comparative advantage in textiles, textile yarn and thread, or clothing. It had been losing comparative advantage in these industries compared to the NICs and ASEAN. In synthetic and regenerated fibres Japan was still leading. In electrical and electronic home appliances, Japan's lead was rapidly being eroded by the ASEAN countries and NICs. In electrical and electronic parts and components, Japan still enjoyed comparative advantage in world markets, but in the key subsector of semiconductor assembly the ASEAN countries already had an advantage against Japan, and the NICs were restructuring to shift from assembly to design and fabrication work.[14] In industrial electrical and electronic machinery Japan enjoyed rising comparative advantage but the other two groups of countries were catching up. In most heavy-industry subsectors, Japan led the other countries by a large margin, but the NICs had overtaken Japan in iron and steel secondary products and finished products.

While the Japanese yen appreciated sharply against the US dollar after 1985, the currencies of Korea and Taiwan were virtually unrevalued in relation to the dollar so that they depreciated considerably against the yen and against European currencies (Table 3.4). Subsequently the Korean and Taiwanese currencies have drifted upwards against the dollar, but the change has been rather gradual. This means that the Asian NICs have become more competitive in the world markets compared to Japan. And this is especially significant in industries such as consumer and industrial electronics where the NICs were already competing fiercely with Japan before the rise of the yen.

The Japan Economic White Paper (1986–1987) noted that the reduction in crude oil prices after 1985 had also been favourable to Korea and Taiwan, and estimated that these two economies would continue along the path of export-led economic growth despite recent upward adjustments to their currencies. Other official publications dealing with the industrial restructuring of Japan emphasize that "... [through] numerous technological innovations

Figure 3.1
RCA changes in Japan, ASEAN and the Asian NICs, 1970–1979

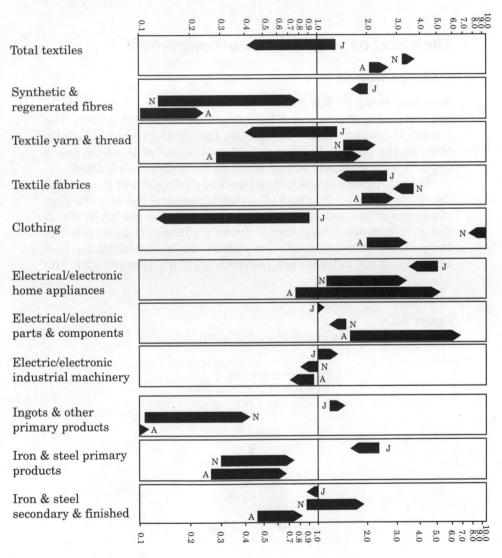

J represents Japan.
N represents the NICs (Korea, Hong Kong, Singapore).
A represents ASEAN (Thailand, Malaysia, Indonesia, Philippines).

SOURCE: Watanabe and Kajiwara (1983).

... the Asian NICs are catching up with Japan" (MITI 1988*b*, p. 167).

The impact on small and medium enterprises[15]

Production networks[16]

Japanese firms do not usually produce everything from parts to final assembly in one vertically integrated industrial system. The parent company which assembles the final products usually controls the design. But the actual production of the final goods depends on a system of labour division through subcontracting.

Three types of subcontract network are prevalent in the production structure. The first sort of network concerns the procurement of raw materials and machinery. The second concerns R&D, which the core company may source from an institution within the company, or from an institution run by the government, another company or an independent research institute (Figure 3.2). The

Figure 3.2
Supply network of Japanese manufacturing industries

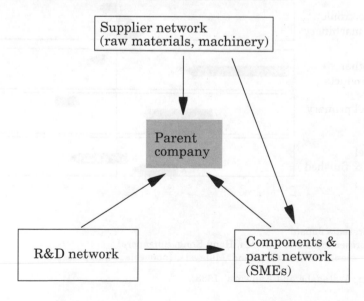

third involves the suppliers of parts and components for final assembly. This third network has been radically affected by the rise of the yen.

Each parent company is supplied by numerous suppliers of parts and components. For example Toyota Motors has about 2,000 major subcontractors supplying parts and components for the motor car assembly plants. Most of the production subcontractors are small and medium enterprises (SMEs), employing less than 300 workers and capitalized at less than 100 million yen. Each major subcontractor may have its own subnetwork of smaller firms. The parent company and the subcontractors are financially independent but they may have links with regards to technical collaboration.

The subcontractors are dependent on parent companies for production expansion, as well as for assistance in R&D. Parent firms are able to obtain high quality products because of the subcontractors' specialization and reliability. The system suits parent firms in another way. The subcontracting system enables efficient division of functions through horizontal subdivision of production processes. The SMEs enjoy greater flexibility in labour management (making use of part-time and casual workers) and other aspects of management compared to the large-scale enterprises. Thus they have been able to keep costs low, which in turn benefits the parent company. Parent companies can also avoid many of the inefficiencies associated with the running of a large integrated industrial system. This industrial structure makes for greater flexibility in technological development and greater resilience in the face of cost and volume adjustments compared to a more integrated industrial system found in the United States and elsewhere. But for the system to work efficiently, subcontractors must usually be located close to their prospective customers. Parent companies and their ancillary subcontractor firms tend to cluster together.

In 1986, SMEs accounted for 87 per cent of all the manufacturing firms and 29 per cent of total manufacturing employment. Some SMEs are independent producers, particularly in light manufacturing subsectors such as toys, garments, cosmetics, food processing and rubber products. But most SMEs are involved in the subcontract system. In 1981, two-thirds of SMEs were involved in subcontracting.

Impact of the yen

As the yen rose, manufacturing production in Japan fell, especially in the SME sector mainly as a result of falling export orders. Industries which exported over 30 per cent of their output were seriously affected. These were, in order of affliction: iron and steel; electrical appliances; transport and shipbuilding; general machinery; and chemicals (MITI 1988*b*).

In 1987, the Small and Medium Enterprise[s] Agency conducted a special survey to enumerate cases of bankruptcy, closure and business suspension in traditional producing regions in the previous two years, with a special focus on export-oriented enterprises. As a proportion of the total number of SMEs, the number of firms in trouble was not very large. With the help of the government and semi-government organizations, the SMEs were able to adjust themselves to the changed economic situations. Strategies for survival included: development of new products; shift to domestic sales; upgrading or adding extra value to the product; reducing the cost of production by rationalization, and lowering the unit purchase price of raw materials (MITI 1988*b*).

The unemployment rate increased marginally from 2.7 per cent in September 1985 to 2.9 per cent in September 1986, and then remained constant through 1987. Unemployment was marginally higher in the traditional parts of the manufacturing sector such as steel, ceramics, metal tableware and textiles. But projections indicate that even in these areas unemployment will fall below 3 per cent within the next five years because the manufacturing industries which are losing their competitive edge are shifting rapidly to the production of more sophisticated products to supply the rapidly expanding domestic market. In some cases, SMEs have actively profited from the high yen, either by reaping the benefits of the lower cost of imported inputs (including oil), or by expanding into the lucrative business of trading in the newly cheap and attractive imported items.

"Escape the influence of the yen!"

While the main methods for adjusting to the change in the industrial structure have been to develop new products, add more value to existing products, shift to domestic sales, or rationalize production costs (in that order), another avenue for export-oriented firms is to relocate production overseas.

Since the yen appreciation, it has become uneconomic to keep many assembly processes in Japan, even those supplying the domestic market. More Japanese conglomerates, their suppliers as well as independent export firms have had to move their operations overseas in order to reduce the cost of production and to remain competitive in the world market.

Japanese firms have been adjusting to a gradually appreciating yen since the mid-1970s. The appreciation of the yen increased the price of the final product in the world market. The parent companies first reacted by trying to force down the costs of components and parts supplied by subcontractors so that they could keep the price of the final product competitive in world markets. But there was always a limit to such cost-cutting and sooner or later the parent firm faced a decline in external demand. The next solution was to shift the final assembly process to subsidiaries or affiliates in overseas locations with lower labour and other costs. Initially subcontractors supplying parts and components resisted relocation. Since the early 1970s, however, increasing numbers of small export firms have relocated their production overseas. For instance, many small firms manufacturing parts for the electronics and electrical appliance industries moved out from Japan into Korea and Taiwan around the mid-1970s in order to escape rising costs. But as long as the yen was kept low in relation to the US dollar, it was still economical for parent firms to import the parts and assemble the final products in Japan.

In the 1980s, and especially after the rise of the yen and the subsequent rise of the NICs' currencies, some parts production had to be relocated again to lower-cost production sites in ASEAN and elsewhere. Also, some Japanese parent companies now found it necessary to shift final assembly operations of some products out of Japan, sometimes to subsidiary companies in ASEAN originally established to supply the host market under import-substitution conditions, and sometimes to entirely new production sites. These parent companies then encouraged their subcontractors also to shift to the cheaper production location in order to bring down the cost of parts and components, and to maintain the close links with the parent firm. The parent company sometimes virtually forced the subcontractors to relocate. Alternatively the overseas affiliates or subsidiaries of the parent company either started their own production of parts locally, or entered into similar subcontract relationships with local firms on the spot.

From 1978 to 1984, the number of Japanese enterprises setting up subsidiaries or overseas joint ventures was around 800 a year. In 1986, this figure jumped to 1,023 and then to 1,419 in 1987. If we isolate the SME portion, the change is even more dramatic. From 1978 to 1984 the annual average was around 300, but this doubled to 599 in 1986 and almost doubled again to 1,063 in 1987 (Figure 3.3).

Much of the initiative for overseas investment came from individual firms themselves. But the Japanese government banks assisted the SMEs by providing low interest loans for overseas operations and by giving information about overseas locations. JETRO (the Japan External Trade Organization) and the Japan Chamber of Commerce, both with branches all over the world, have been instrumental in facilitating the move overseas among the SMEs.

The new strategy of relocation and export-orientation

After the appreciation of the yen, the strategy of Japanese foreign investment changed. Whereas in the earlier period foreign investment had largely functioned as a means to capture markets for goods made mainly with parts and components manufactured in Japan, after 1985 foreign investment functioned as a means to structure production in the face of increased international competition. ASEAN again became an attractive location for Japanese investors, but for an entirely new set of reasons. Japanese firms needed to relocate production to low-cost sites in order to compete in international markets against new low-cost producers, particularly the Asian NICs. Whereas the earlier strategy had been designed to increase production in Japan, the new strategy could entail an actual transfer of production out of Japan as firms sought to "escape the influence of the yen".

The number of Japanese export-oriented investment projects in ASEAN increased sharply. In Indonesia, the number of new export-oriented projects established by Japanese firms had averaged 3.7 projects per year between 1970 and 1984. Between 1985 and 1987, the average jumped to fourteen a year. In Thailand, the Board of Investment approved 260 Japanese investment projects between 1986 and May 1988. Of these 206, or 79 per cent, were classified as

Figure 3.3
Overseas investments by Japanese enterprises

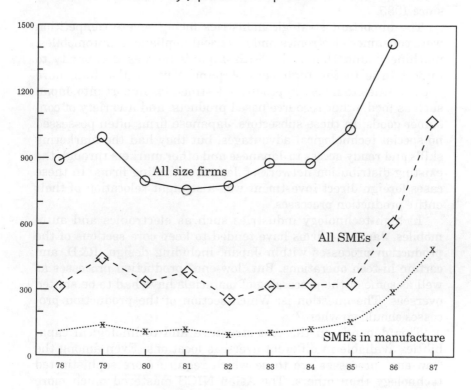

Notes
1. Only new acquisitions of securities (the establishment of local subsidiaries, and the acquisition of equity shares in local enterprises) are covered.
2. Investments by small and medium enterprises include joint investments with large enterprises and private investments.
3. There is no continuity in the statistics because only investments of ¥10 million or more were covered by the statistics from April 1984 instead of investments of ¥3 million or more as in the past.

SOURCES: Enterprises of all scales, Ministry of Finance statistics, and small and medium enterprises, MITI survey.

export industries, namely projects which exported at least 80 per cent of their products. In late 1987, JETRO conducted a survey of Japanese subsidiaries in ASEAN. The majority of the firms surveyed reported increases in their export to Japan in the period since 1985.

The important strategic industries facing severe competition were consumer electronics and electrical appliances, automobiles, machinery, and chemicals. With Japan's increased capacity to import (due to the high yen), Japanese firms also had more opportunities to invest in products destined for import into Japan such as food, other resource based products, and a variety of consumer goods. In these subsectors, Japanese firms often possessed no special technological advantages, but they had the marketing skills and ready access to Japanese and other markets through the existing distribution network of Japanese trading firms. In these cases foreign direct investment was a straight relocation of their entire production processes.

In high-technology industries such as electronics and automobiles, Japanese firms have tended to keep core sections of the production processes within Japan, including design, R&D, and certain hi-tech operations. But "low-end" production processes as well as some of the processing of materials have had to be shifted overseas. The question is: Which section of the production processes should go where?

This depends on the cost structure and technological capabilities available in different overseas locations. Even among the "low-end" processes are those which require more sophisticated technology than others. The Asian NICS mastered much more sophisticated production techniques than the ASEAN countries, and thus are still important as suppliers of some sophisticated parts and components (such as in the case of electronics and automobiles). Investment in the production of parts and components is still growing in these countries.

Within ASEAN, different countries are at different stages of technological advance, and so each has attracted a different mix of manufacturing investment from Japan in the period after 1985.[16]

For Singapore and Malaysia, new Japanese investment has been concentrated in electronics. Between 1986 and 1987, according to JETRO, Japanese firms set up twenty-three semiconductor companies in these two countries. Singapore developed into the hub of the electronics industry in the region. By offering new tax breaks to companies wishing to set up regional operational headquarters (OHQ), the Singapore Government attracted several electronics multinationals, and in return for the tax breaks, demanded that the multinationals must locate their regional R&D, distribution centre, financial system and service network in Singapore. The attractiveness of the tax offer and the availability of good infrastructure such as an efficient communications network and good port facilities, essential for the transportation of parts and components of electronics products, have induced not only Japanese electronic firms (Sony, Matsushita), but also American (Data General) and German (Nixdorf) firms to obtain OHQ status.

Singapore's established position as a trade and service centre has also attracted Japanese investment in trade, banking and other services. In 1987 and the first four months of 1988, JETRO Singapore recorded 89 cases of Japanese investment in foreign trade and commerce and another 40 cases of Japanese investment in other services.

The three main factors attracting Japanese firms to Thailand are low labour costs, the availability of many raw materials (such as fishery products, rubber) and the existence of local entrepreneurs ready to enter into strategic alliances with Japanese firms. Low labour costs and entrepreneur alliances attracted Japanese investment into five joint-venture projects to produce automotive parts and components for export, and into several projects in low-end consumer electronics, again mainly for export. Electronics firms from the United States, Singapore and Taiwan have set up factories in Thailand for the same reasons. Low labour costs combined with resource availability attracted Japanese investment into ventures in food processing, wooden furniture, machine tools, chemicals and other intermediate products.

In Indonesia, new Japanese investment went into food, fishery, textiles, and chemicals (for exports). And in the Philippines, there were some Japanese investment in electronics and automobile parts manufacturing.

Japanese investment and new networks in ASEAN

While the nature of investment varied greatly from country to country, there are examples of greater industrial integration emerging across ASEAN under the aegis of Japanese investment.

Some Japanese firms are building up pan-Asian networks through foreign investment in collaboration with their affiliates, and through marketing links with non-Japanese companies. The purpose of these networks is to ensure a supply of low cost components and parts outside Japan.

This is clearly seen in the case of some electrical appliance firms in the region. Figure 3.4 shows the network of foreign investments of AIWA, a 100 per cent subsidiary of Sony specializing in audio and video equipment, and its relationships with affiliates or subsidiaries across ASEAN. In its Singapore base, AIWA now assembles 50 per cent of its global output, sourcing 75 per cent of the parts from other Japanese firms in Singapore and Malaysia, and the remaining 25 per cent of high-tech parts from Japan, or from Japanese firms located in Taiwan and Korea.

Figure 3.4
Production network of AIWA

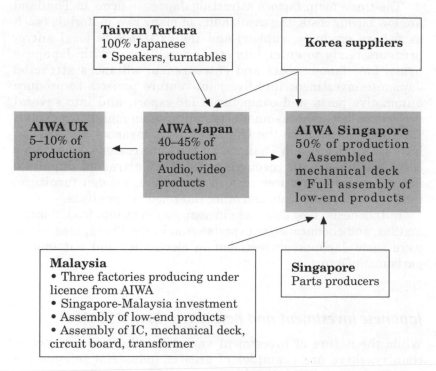

SOURCE: Based on the author's interview with AIWA, Singapore, September 1988.

Sharp has built up a similarly complex network of affiliates and subsidiaries across the region. Sharp set up three joint-venture companies in Malaysia: one producing TV receivers for domestic sale and for export; one producing only for domestic sale, and the third producing electronic components and parts for export only. Sharp also has subsidiaries in Thailand, Taiwan, and Singapore. The plants in Malaysia produce most of the parts they require, but also import some of the hi-tech components from Sharp in Japan and Taiwan, while other parts are sourced from affiliates of Sharp in Malaysia itself, and from other electronic firms in Singapore and Malaysia. The plants assembling for export were recently established following the pressure of the rising yen.[17]

These export platforms of Sharp and AIWA were established in ASEAN very recently, but some Japanese firms producing parts and components have been set up in ASEAN and Asian NICs since the late 1970s. Initially they manufactured parts and components for export to final assembly plants in Japan. Since the yen appreciation, these firms have also started to undertake final assembly and to export the finished products to Japan and elsewhere.[18]

Similar networks are found in the automotive industry. The Mitsubishi group, for instance, sources automobile parts and components from a network of affiliates and subsidiaries in Thailand, Malaysia, the Philippines, Indonesia, and also Canada and Australia. All five major Japanese automotive producers have formed networks of affiliates and subsidiaries which span ASEAN and the Asian NICs (Figure 3.5). It has been speculated that more Japanese automobile firms may be forced to relocate more of their production for exports to the ASEAN region in the near future, partly because of the local content requirements laid down by the local governments, and partly because of increased competition from Korean and Taiwanese firms adopting a similar strategy.

As Japanese companies started to network their production processes across ASEAN, they became more interested in the concept of ASEAN as a common market. As Dr Mahathir pointed out, foreign investors and traders have shown more enthusiasm than member countries for the concept of ASEAN as an economic unit.[19] So far much of the initiative to induce ASEAN member countries to reduce tariff barriers, to consider industrial co-operation schemes, or to think about the concept of a common market have come mainly from outside, especially from foreign investors and traders.

Since the 1970s, the Japanese Government and private

Figure 3.5
Japanese auto makers and affiliates in Asia, 1986

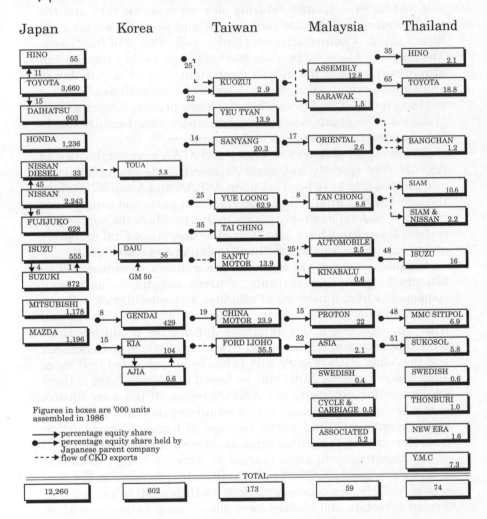

Figures in boxes are '000 units
assembled in 1986

→ percentage equity share
●→ percentage equity share held by Japanese parent company
- - -→ flow of CKD exports

SOURCE: S. Kikuchi, "International Relations between Japan, Asian NICs and
ASEAN in Machinery Industry with Special Reference to Automobile and
Electronic Industries" in *Survey*, Japan Development Bank, May 1988 (in
Japanese).

Japanese investors have pushed for several industrial co-operation schemes involving Japanese direct investment or technological tie-ups. The main feature of these schemes is reduced tariff rates on goods moved between ASEAN member countries. The schemes are not geared exclusively to Japanese investors, but given the geographical proximity and the interest shown both by the Japanese Government and by Japanese investors, it is very likely that Japanese investors would play an important role in these schemes.[20]

Two of the early schemes, the ASEAN Industrial Projects (AIP) and the ASEAN Industrial Complementation scheme (AIC), were based on recommendations contained in the Kansu Report, prepared by the United Nations in 1972 (Chng 1985). The AIP scheme aimed to set up large-scale government-initiated industrial projects which could utilize raw materials of member countries, create employment and contribute to economic growth. Prime Minister Fukuda of Japan committed soft loans of US$1 billion to fund the projects.[21]

In 1980, these schemes were superseded by the ASEAN Industrial Joint Ventures (AIJV) scheme, which M.K. Chng describes as "private sector equivalents of AIPs enjoying exclusivity and other privileges ... but with various added elements of flexibility" (Chng 1985, p. 43). To qualify as an AIJV, a project had to have at least 40 per cent ASEAN ownership.[22] The benefits included a halving of tariffs on intra-regional trade in components between units of the same manufacturer. Up to 1988, twenty-one AIJV projects had been approved.[23] Most of the projects had foreign investment components, with Japanese investors in the automobile, motor cycle and machinery industries playing an important role.[24]

Japanese investment and increase in local content

With the rise of the yen, Japanese firms located in ASEAN which previously relied heavily on supply of parts and components made in Japan were obliged to look around for cheaper, local sources of supply. As we have seen, this resulted in many Japanese sub-contract firms relocating to ASEAN in order to continue to supply their parent firm. This was common in the electronics industry as the AIWA example cited above shows. But local sourcing is not confined to Japanese affiliates. AIWA in Malaysia subcontracts to local firms to make parts under licence.

There is no hard data on the extent of local sourcing, but a survey carried out by JETRO in late 1987 indicated increased local content among Japanese subsidiaries. The survey covered a sample of 400 Japanese firms operating in the five ASEAN countries. A quarter of the sample were 100 per cent Japanese subsidiaries, another two-thirds were joint ventures with host country capital, and the remainder were joint ventures between Japanese capital and third country capital (JETRO 1988). The survey asked the sample firms to compare the level of local content (the proportion of parts and components procured from local producers as distinct from imported parts) at the time of the survey in late 1987 to the situation before the yen appreciation in 1985 (Tables 3.5 and 3.6).

Table 3.5
Distribution of Japanese affiliates in ASEAN by ratio of local content
(In percentages)

	>70	50–70	<50	Total	
Food	55.5	18.5	26.0	100	(27)
Textiles	19.1	27.7	53.2	100	(47)
Wood products	100.0	–	–	100	(8)
Petroleum and chemical products	33.9	17.9	48.2	100	(56)
Metal and non-metallic products	28.9	13.2	57.9	100	(38)
General machinery	28.3	10.5	63.2	100	(19)
Electrical machinery and electronics	16.0	24.5	59.4	100	(106)
Transport equipment	14.3	19.6	66.1	100	(56)
Others	33.3	16.7	50.0	100	(54)
Total	26.8	19.7	53.5	100	(411)

SOURCE: JETRO, *Report of a Survey on Conditions of Japanese Affiliates in ASEAN,* Tokyo, March 1988, in Japanese.

Table 3.6
Changes in the ratio of local content among Japanese affiliates
in the ASEAN, August 1987 compared with the period before
September 1985
(In percentages)

	Increase substantially	No change	Decrease	Total
Food	16.7	75.0	8.3	100 (24)
Textile	40.5	59.5	0	100 (37)
Wood products	14.3	85.7	0	100 (7)
Petroleum and chemical products	51.8	48.2	0	100 (56)
Metal and non-metallic products	35.1	62.2	2.7	100 (37)
General machinery	58.8	41.2	0	100 (17)
Electrical machinery and electronics	69.2	28.6	2.2	100 (91)
Transport equipment	55.6	44.4	0	100 (45)
Others	57.4	42.6	0	100 (47)
Total	51.8	46.8	1.4	100 (361)

SOURCE: JETRO, *Report of a Survey on Conditions of Japanese Affiliates in ASEAN* (Tokyo, March 1988), in Japanese.

Just over a quarter of the firms which answered the question reported that they now used over 70 per cent local content, a fifth was in the range of 50 to 70 per cent and over half had less than 50 per cent local content. Firms with the highest ratio of local content were concentrated in resource-based industries such as wood products and petrochemicals.

Over half of the firms (361 answered this question) reported that the ratio of the local content in their operation had increased substantially since 1985. The increases were marked in electrical machinery and electronics, general machinery and transport equipment, petrochemicals, textiles and the unclassified industries.

Table 3.7
Reasons for increased purchase of parts and components from firms in host countries among Japanese affiliates in ASEAN, 1987[a]

Reasons	Indonesia	Malaysia	Philippines	Singapore	Thailand
Quality of local products improve	14	11	0	20	15
Find suitable supplies	29	19	2	36	31
Increased production of parts themselves	17	0	2	11	13
Invite part makers from Japan	1	3	0	3	3
Increase purchase of parts from affiliates within host country	13	12	0	25	8
Prices of local supplies fall	4	0	1	7	0
Production ability of local firms improves	5	0	0	5	3
Guidance of host government improves local firms' performance	17	0	0	1	7
Others	3	0	1	6	0

a Multiple answers

SOURCE: JETRO, *Report of a Survey on Conditions of Japanese Affiliates in ASEAN* (Tokyo, March 1988), in Japanese.

The JETRO survey also asked how the firms had managed to increase the level of local content. Although relatively few firms managed to answer the question, the largest number of answers indicated greater success in sourcing parts from local firms mainly because the quality of products available from local firms had improved, in some cases with assistance from the host governments (Table 3.7). In other cases the firms either had expanded into parts production themselves, or were sourcing more from other Japanese firms located in the host country. Of the three methods (local supply, own production, other Japanese firms), over two-thirds of the answers referred to increased local content sourced from local firms owned by domestic capital.

The quality of the survey results depends on how well respondent firms co-operate. The response rate was good: nearly half of the sample returned the questionnaire. Although not all respondents completed all the questions, the questions were simple enough so we can assume there was little distortion due to misunderstanding. To this extent we can say that the survey results show that Japanese investment after 1985 has involved an increase in local content in ASEAN.

Changes in the local content of items produced by foreign manu-facturers are generally an indication of technology transfer. Foreign firms will only substitute locally-made parts for those imported from the home base or other developed countries when they believe the locally-made items meet their standards of quality. For local entrepreneurs, the opportunity to supply parts to a Japa-nese or other foreign-venture firm can be highly significant as the subcontract arrangement may involve some technical assistance from the parent firm.

The development of Japanese firms overseas

In the 1960s, the typical agent of Japanese overseas investment was the Sogo Shosha, the large and diversified Japanese trading company which became involved in investment projects as an essential part of its basic import-export business role. Through the 1970s, the role of the Sogo Shosha gradually diminished, as individual Japanese manufacturing firms established their own independent networks and subsidiaries overseas. Initially such overseas operations were confined mostly to sales and sourcing operations.

More recently, the operational scope of overseas subsidiaries of Japanese firms has greatly expanded. From sales and sourcing operations, they developed into production bases. At the same time, the parent firm generally retained R&D, marketing control, and finance at headquarters in Japan. This became the typical pattern of the emergent Japanese multinational company of the 1980s.

At the same time, certain companies are already developing beyond this stage. As described in the previous section, some firms are developing interlocking networks linking overseas subsidiaries in a production complex. Others are following the earlier pattern of United States multinationals in devolving more operational

autonomy to regional and even local levels.[25] Sony has established
a regional headquarters, including R&D laboratories, in Singapore.
As part of a worldwide strategy of "global localization", Matsushita
is grouping its sixty-nine overseas plants under four regional
headquarters, one of which is also in Singapore.

Besides new organizational forms, Japanese interests overseas
also display new modes of operation. Nakakita (1988) has focused
attention on forms of overseas Japanese involvement which differ
from the conventional style of direct investment. These forms
include technology contracts, management contracts, franchise
arrangements, turnkey projects, and production sharing, sometimes in return for a minority equity share in the enterprise. He
classified these new forms of investment into three types: business
tie-ups, which largely involve sales arrangements for brand name
goods; technology tie-ups, which largely involve licensing of
technology or co-operative arrangements for R&D, and production
co-operation, which largely means commission and licensing
arrangements (1988, p. 309).

Studies by Chee and Lee (1979) and Allen (1979) found that
new multinationals from Japan have engaged in this new form of
investment much more readily than American firms. Nakakita
(1988) found the new forms of investment by Japanese firms in the
period after 1985 to be most prevalent in the United States, Europe
and the Asian NICs. However even in ASEAN they showed signs of
rapid increase. To overcome the fact that such forms of investment
are not properly monitored by conventional investment statistics,
Nakakita made a simple count of such projects mentioned in the
press between 1985 and 1988. In the first half of 1988, almost a
third of all Japanese investment projects in ASEAN were of this
type.[26]

The increasing importance of the new form of investment
among Japanese multinational corporations reflects the increased
maturity of the Japanese economy and Japanese firms. As Japanese firms are forced to become more global to survive, they
increasingly seek out diversified ways of exploiting their accumulated human capital, technical innovations, and expertise in
management and marketing in various ways other than foreign
direct investment. The growing incidence of these "new forms" of
investment in ASEAN signifies the increased role of firm-specific
advantages as a determinant of Japanese direct investment in the
region.[27] According to Nakakita, these new forms of investment

indicate the opportunities available to Japanese firms to market their accumulated assets by way of managerial resources, organizational technique, and command of information.

Summary

Up to 1985, Japanese investment in ASEAN was concentrated in resource extraction and import substitution. The relocation of export-oriented industries out of Japan had largely focused on the NICs and had only to a small extent affected ASEAN. Since 1985 the scale of foreign investment flowing into the region has risen sharply and is projected to grow even faster in the coming years. Moreover there has been a transformation in the nature of Japanese investment. Now it flows largely into manufacturing parts and finished products for export to Japan and world markets.

The new wave of investment occurred following the rise in the yen, but both the investment flow and the currency adjustment need to be interpreted as results of the transformation of the Japanese economy and its relationship to the world. In two decades, Japan has been transformed from a low-wage economy concentrated in heavy industry, to an economy focused on high-technology industry and services with rapidly rising wage rates. In response to the oil crises of the 1970s, Japan invested heavily in improving productivity and energy-saving, while depressing the yen to retain international competitiveness. The strategy was massively successful in enabling Japan to build export markets, largely in the developed world. When the currency finally had to be revalued and wage rates allowed to rise, Japan no longer possessed comparative advantage in the manufacture of many items which had generated her export revenue in recent years. Many Japanese firms were obliged to relocate in order to remain competitive in the face of competitors and imitators from the West and from the NICs.

In the period before the mid-1980s, most Japanese manufacturers relocating to ASEAN were final producers assembling for the local market. Now several of these firms have been transformed into export producers supplying both the Japanese home market and third-country markets. Meanwhile, many SMEs producing parts and components for these final producers were obliged to relocate closer to the parent. In certain industries, networks of subcontractors and final producers have emerged spanning across the ASEAN region. As well as attracting their subcontract firms to relocate from Japan, many Japanese firms located in the region have found it profitable to source more parts and components from local subcontract firms. In addition, many Japanese firms have begun to experiment with new forms of investment through which they can market their accumulated assets of managerial resources, technology, brand names and information reserves as alternatives to conventional direct investment.

In sum, as the Japanese economy matured, it acquired comparative advantage in high-tech areas and shifted the structure of the economy in Japan in this direction. At the same time, Japan lost comparative advantage in many of the production processes on which Japanese firms had built their prosperity in the past two decades. Japanese firms cannot remain competitive in world markets if they continue to locate these production processes in Japan. However, they possess many specific advantages which can continue to deliver competitive advantages in world markets as long as the production base is shifted to locations with better comparative advantage in terms of resource provision. Some of the specific advantages wielded by Japanese firms derive from vertical linkages back to the high-tech heart of the Japanese economy. However, many advantages are derived from the "intangible assets" of the firm in the form of management resources, control of information, and marketing tools that include brand name franchises. In this respect, Japanese firms are coming to resemble the American multinationals. And like the American multinationals, they are being drawn to regionalize and localize their multinational operations to be able to best exploit their specific advantages in varied local environments. Rather more than American multinationals, however, they are experimenting with new forms of investment which maximize returns to these specific advantages.

Up to now, the discussion has focused on the motivations driving capital out of Japan, and on the strategies Japanese firms have adopted to remain competitive in the world markets of the late 1980s. The analysis in this chapter shows that while the rise of the yen triggered the new exodus of Japanese capital, the more fundamental causes of the large influx of Japanese investment into ASEAN after 1985 lay in the structural changes within the Japanese economy. This is the important factor on the supply side. But the analysis will not be complete without looking at the demand side, at the propensity of the host ASEAN countries to attract conventional foreign direct investment as well as the new forms of investment.

Almost exactly a decade before the Group of Five meeting which started the rise of the yen, the ruling Japanese prime minister, Tanaka, toured the ASEAN countries and became the focus for a violent outpouring of popular resentment against Japanese economic penetration. The new wave of investment is much larger in scale than those of the mid-1970s. Yet so far there are no signs of similar resentment. Indeed between 1985 and 1988, ASEAN governments rewrote policies on foreign investment in order to roll out the red carpet for the Japanese.

The scale of the new foreign investment in ASEAN cannot be explained solely in terms of the strategies of the overseas investors alone. The receptivity of the ASEAN states needs to be analysed.

Notes

1. Apart from works by Japanese writers cited earlier in Chapter 2, other works on the old wave from which information in this section is derived include Allen (1973a), Seiji Naya and Akrasanee (1974), Sekiguchi and Krause (1980), Thee (1984a), and Hill (1988).
2. Information is from MITI as reported in Phongpaichit (1988).
3. Singapore is the exception.
4. These figures must be used with caution as they are the figures reported to the Ministry of Finance. Not all the projects reported will be realized in the same year. Some may not get off the ground, while projects planned and reported earlier may be realized in the year in question. To this extent, the figures are best used as trends. Further-more, the value of new Japanese investment may be an overestimate when compared to the figures of earlier years as the latter were not adjusted for price changes. On the other hand the figures of new Japa-nese investment may be an underestimate because they do not include projects by overseas subsidiaries which obtained the requisite money from abroad. See Nakakita (1988), p. 309. It should also be noted that in yen terms the new investment, as reported by the Ministry of Finance, did not increase as much as in dollar terms because of the yen appreciation, and the absolute amount in yen values declined between 1985 and 1986. The value of Japanese direct investment into ASEAN in billions of yen were 215.2, 223.0, 144.1 and 222.4 respectively for 1984, 1985, 1986 and 1987 (using the data in Tables 3.1 and 3.4.). It could be argued however that the consistently high level of Japanese direct investment (except in 1986) was very important to ASEAN

countries in that it came at the time of the slowing down of the inflow of investment from other developed countries, and also at the time of low economic growth rates in ASEAN.

5. See the section entitled "The new strategy of relocation and export-orientation" below.

6. In the period 1977–85, total direct foreign investment was a small fraction of gross domestic capital formation in Indonesia, the Philippines and Thailand, namely 0.65, 1.69 and 1.30 per cent respectively. But foreign investment was more significant in Malaysia and Singapore and accounted respectively for 10.93 and 17.34 per cent of gross domestic capital formation for the same period. See James, Naya and Meier (1987), Table 4.11, p. 138.

7. Estimates based on a method used by the Pacific Rim Consultancy Group.

8. See for example Seichi Tsukasaki, "Japanese Direct Investment Abroad", *Journal of Japanese Trade and Industry* 6, no. 4, 1987.

9. This section draws upon the following works: Bix (1982), Ng, Hirono and Akrasanee (1987), Thorn (1988), Chen (1988, 1989), Economic Planning Agency, Japan (1987), Ozawa (1985).

10. Many of these workers come from South Korea, Pakistan and Bangladesh. For the last two countries, Japan had a reciprocal visa agreement until mid-January 1989. The Immigration Bureau, Ministry of Justice has estimated the number of illegal migrants working as unskilled workers to be around 70,000 in 1988. The figure is expected to reach 100,000 and beyond in the near future. Professionals and highly skilled workers in short supply in Japan, such as financial experts, computer specialists and English teachers, are allowed to migrate legally. This information is from an interview with officials of the Immigration Bureau in Tokyo in 1988.

11. The Japanese Government supported export industries by giving priority across the board in the allocation of financial capital. This was achieved by setting the rate of interest for export firms below the market clearing level and by rationing credit through the banking system and specialized government financial institutions. See Suzuki (1980).

12. This section draws on the following works: Chen (1988), Ng, Hirono and Akrasanee (1987), MITI (1988*b*) and the author's fieldwork in Japan in 1986 and in 1988.

13. The information in Figure 3.1 should be used with caution, as it is highly aggregated. The figures at best show a broad indication of trends.

14. Several semiconductor assembly plants have recently been shifted from the NICs to new locations in ASEAN, especially Malaysia and Thailand.

15. This section draws upon the author's fieldwork in Japan in 1986 (see

Phongpaichit [1988]) and in 1988, as well as the following works: Kunasirin (1987), Chen (1988), Imai (1988), MITI (1988). The author also benefited greatly from discussions with Mr Seiki Teshiba of Nomura Research Institute, Mr Masuyuki Sueda of JETRO Singapore, Mr Takashi Torii of IDE and interviews of Japanese joint-venture firms in Indonesia, Singapore and Thailand in 1988.

16. The information is from JETRO, and from the records of approved foreign investment of each ASEAN country.

17. The author would like to thank Takashi Torii of IDE Tokyo for sharing the information about Sharp. See also Torii (1988).

18. Sony has a similar kind of network. But Sony has now set up a regional headquarters in Singapore (Sony International). One of the functions of Sony International is to purchase parts and components of electronic products for all its subsidiaries for the final assembly. This centralized function reduces the overhead costs of purchasing operations. Many other electronics multinationals have set up similar kinds of operations in Singapore.

19. See Mahathir (1987).

20. See details and history of the schemes in Chng (1985), and chapters by Chee and others in Sopiee (1987).

21. The AIP ran into problems and was replaced by the AIC, but neither project had much success. See Chang (1985) for a review of the state of affairs and difficulties involved.

22. Initially the ASEAN ownership share was set at 51 per cent, but in October 1988 this was reduced to 40 per cent for nominations received up to December 1990.

23. Ten from Malaysia, five from Thailand, four from Indonesia and one each from the Philippines and Singapore.

24. AIJV has met with more success than other schemes largely because of initiatives from the private sector. Interviews with interested foreign investors suggest that they are still facing many problems from the bureaucratic procedures of the ASEAN Secretariat and individual ASEAN country members. This is evidence of weak demand from the ASEAN side.

25. See "The Multinational, Eastern Style" in *The Economist*, 24 June 1989.

26. In the first half of 1988, Nakakita counted 40 cases of the "new forms" in ASEAN out of a total of 126 cases. For comparison, the number of new form cases in the NICs was 113 out of a total of 192 (Nakakita 1988, Table IV, p. 310).

27. There is also a demand-side aspect to the increase in these new forms, which is not properly recognized by analysts such as Nakakita. See Chapter 4 below.

4

The ASEAN perspective of Japanese investment

Much of the theoretical and empirical work on foreign investment
focused closely on supply motivations. Where conditions in the host
country were included in the analysis, they tended to be interpreted from the viewpoint of the investor country, in terms of "pull"
factors or even more generally as the "investment climate". In some
such writings, there was also an implicit assumption that foreign
investment was desirable for the host developing country, and the
analysis was directed towards advising prospective host countries
how best to attract foreign investors.[1] These studies analysed
conditions in host countries in categories like political stability,
incentive policies, availability of necessary manpower, infrastructure, and support industries. These were factors which made
the host country attractive to the foreign investor. They were quite
different from factors which determined the demand for foreign
investment from the host country's side.

Similarly, the appearance of "new forms of investment" by Japanese firms has tended to be analysed wholly from the supply angle.
According to this approach, Japanese firms undertook these "new
forms" in order to maximize returns on their accumulated specific

advantages. There has been little attempt to analyse the extent to which the appearance of new forms can be linked to the desire of governments and domestic capital in host countries to gain access to technology and other advantages possessed by Japanese firms without ceding equity share or management control.[2]

This chapter analyses the demand for foreign capital in the ASEAN states. The first section sets out a general framework for discussing the demand for foreign capital. This is followed by an overview of factors affecting the demand for foreign capital over the period from the 1950s to the early 1980s. The third section examines the impact of the recession of the early 1980s on government, and the fourth section summarizes the resulting changes in official regulations concerning foreign investment. The final section traces changes in the attitudes of domestic capital towards foreign capital inflow.

Domestic capital, state capital, foreign capital[3]

In any country at any time, the key factors affecting the demand for foreign capital are the attitude of domestic capital, and the attitude of government, with respect to what they see as benefits and costs to be derived from foreign investment.

In certain circumstances, domestic capital may view foreign capital as a threat, as a competitor. It may then put pressure on government to restrict the inflow, refuse to co-operate in joint projects, and otherwise disrupt or deter foreign investment. In other circumstances, domestic capital may see foreign capital as an ally, a source of technology and strength, and may therefore influence government to facilitate the inflow, and co-operate willingly. Whether domestic capital is warm or cool towards foreign capital is likely to be determined by two main factors: its estimate of the relative strength of domestic versus foreign capital, and its estimate of the extent to which government will protect and promote the interest of domestic capital in the face of foreign competition.

As for the government, there are three main sets of factors shaping its attitude to foreign capital: first, the government's assessment of the impact foreign capital will have on the economy as a whole; second, its assessment of the impact of foreign investment on the government's own economic interests, namely state capital,

and third, its assessment of the impact of foreign investment on
the political balance, particularly on the political role of domestic
capital.

In order to maintain itself in power the state must ensure a flow
of revenue, which it can use for defence, for economic and social
development, and for satisfying the demands of its power base. The
revenue flows better if the economy is growing. All the ASEAN
states aim to promote industrialization under a free enterprise
system as a means to achieve economic growth. Their attitude towards foreign investment will thus be affected by their analysis of
the extent to which foreign capital can promote growth, enhance
state revenue, and foster the stability of the regime.

Besides this general state interest, there is also the more
specific state interest bound up with state capital. In many developing countries, including those of ASEAN, the state plays an
active role in capital accumulation through state enterprises and
government participation in joint public-private ventures. Just like
domestic capital, this "state capital" interest can view foreign
capital as a threat or as a source of strength, depending on
circumstance.[4]

In addition, the state's attitude to foreign investment will be
affected by its assessment of the impact of foreign capital on the
interests which support its maintenance of power. The state must
be responsive towards different social groups which provide the
state with a base of support. This is rather obvious in the case of a
democratically elected government which must always be sensitive
to the need for re-election. But it is equally true in non-democratic
situations. This factor can be especially important for military
regimes whose success and survival often depend on the continued
prosperity and support of small groups and factions. Such regimes
must always gauge what impact foreign capital is likely to have on
the factional balance.

In trying to maintain its objectives, the state will often face
fundamental constraints on its policy options because the interests
of domestic capital, foreign capital and the state itself are in
conflict. For instance, private domestic and foreign capital may
want a more liberal economic framework, while the government
may prefer to maintain tighter controls either to facilitate revenue-
gathering or to facilitate political favouritism in the award of
business opportunities. In a more general context, state support of
large multinationals may upset small local enterprises who feel

threatened by competition from foreign firms. For these reasons, policy towards foreign investment is rarely simple and straight-forward. Indeed often it is riven with self-contradiction and compromise. This makes it especially hard to analyse, and some simplification is necessary. The next section will examine how, in the period from the 1960s to the mid-1980s, the attitudes of governments and domestic business moulded the demand for foreign investment in each country.

State, domestic and foreign capital in ASEAN up to 1985[5]

From the 1960s to the early 1980s, the ASEAN governments were, as a general rule, rather lukewarm toward foreign investment. In this period, state capital in most of the countries was expanding its scale and influence, and was not keen to allow foreign capital to enter as a competitor into its own areas of interest. At the same time, governments could recognize that foreign capital could con-tribute benefits, particularly new technology, additional employ-ment, and raised efficiency levels, in domestic firms exposed to competition. Thus even in this period when state capital was domi-nant, foreign investment was admitted though usually under restrictive conditions stipulated by the state. Domestic capital was generally opposed to foreign capital inflow and periodically lobbied the state to protect its interests.

While state capital was in the ascendant in all four countries during this period, the development of domestic capital and the relationship between state and domestic capital differed greatly from country to country. In the 1980s, these differences were to affect the receptivity towards foreign capital inflow.

Indonesia

The demand for foreign capital in Indonesia was shaped by one major influence: the existence of a large state capital sector. From the 1960s through to the mid-1980s, state capital was largely opposed to the inflow of foreign capital, which it viewed as a poten-tial threat to its own position. The weak domestic capital sector also did not feel strong enough to bargain profitably with foreign capital and so supported government policies which preserved the domestic market for domestic capital. In the mid-1960s, a foreign exchange crisis coupled with a realignment of internal political forces caused the attitudes towards foreign investment to soften somewhat, but the basic policy orientation remained lukewarm to foreign capital until the mid-1980s.[6]

In 1957, Soekarno's military regime nationalized foreign firms. By 1960, 489 Dutch companies had been nationalized, including 216 in plantations, 161 in industry and mining, 40 in trading, and 16 in insurance (Pangestu and Habir 1989). In 1967 some of the nationalized firms were returned to the previous Dutch, British and American owners, but state capital remained important in public utilities, petroleum, mining, aluminium smelting, fertilizer production, printing, communications, animal husbandry, transport, construction, trade, forestry, fisheries, real estate, cement, pulp and paper (Thee and Yoshihara 1987). In addition, 80 per cent of the bank loans remained under the control of the government, and until the end of 1988, the banking sector was closed to new investment from foreign capital.

Moreover, the importance of state capital was even more pronounced than these statistics of government enterprises suggest. A large number of domestic entrepreneurs were dependent on the state for subcontract work in areas such as construction, and procurement of materials, goods and services. In addition, various departments in the military ran business enterprises. State capital and its allies pervaded the Indonesian economy.

The Soekarno regime was able to push through the nationalization programme in the late 1950s for two reasons. First, the regime had inherited a relatively powerful state structure from the Dutch. Second, the regime drew its support from peasant and labour interests which were very opposed to the old colonial interests and to the Chinese entrepreneurial groups which dominated private capital at the end of the Dutch period. The moderate party which represented the middle class and indigenous petty capitalists tried to persuade the government to transfer some of the ex-Dutch enterprises to the private sector. It was not successful, largely because the candidates to take over these enterprises were mainly Indonesian Chinese who had become identified with Dutch colonial rule. The military governments under Soekarno justified the state role in business as a means to reduce the power of Chinese domestic capital and to develop the country in the interests of the Indonesian nation.

Domestic capital was divided into Pribumi (Indonesian) and

Chinese segments. The Pribumi capitalists tended to be small scale and rather inexperienced. The few medium and large scale enterprises had grown through association with government and were essentially adjuncts of state capital. They relied heavily on subcontract work from state enterprises, and had privileged access to state credit facilities and licences. Chinese capital concentrated on manufacturing production and especially on distribution for the domestic market. Domestic capital lobbied for government to protect the internal market from any inflow of foreign capital. Government responded by more or less protecting domestic distribution, service industries and low-technology manufacturing for the home market.

In the mid-1960s, the Indonesian economy ran into severe problems over the balance of payments. At the same time, the advent of the new Soeharto regime represented an adjustment in the configuration of political forces. The new regime recognized that the spread of state enterprises was only partially successful. It also recognized that Chinese capital was vital to the continued growth and prosperity of the Indonesian economy. To solve the balance-of-payments problem and to sustain growth, the government began to admit more foreign investment and set out to reach a *modus vivendi* with domestic private capital, including the dominant Chinese segment.

The Soeharto regime continued to nurture and extend state capital which provided a major source of revenue for the government and its supporters. And continued to maintain a framework of investment regulations and licensing rules for controlling the development of private capital. But to a greater extent than under the previous regime, Soeharto promoted the growth of selected business interests which harmonized with the interests of state capital and the interests of the regime itself. These selected business interests were both Pribumi and Chinese. As part of this more pragmatic policy-making, the regime was also significantly more open to foreign capital

The government relaxed some of the restrictions on foreign investment, but only partially. The Foreign Investment Law of 1967 provided a structure for admitting foreign investment but still preserved sectors such as public utilities, harbours, shipping, aviation, atomic energy and mass media for state control.[7] Foreign capital was admitted in areas where it offered no serious threat to the interests of the state or to those of favoured domestic capital (meaning businesses which could seek protection from the state, or businesses run by those who were allies of the government in power), and in areas where the country needed the high technology which foreign capital controlled. Even in these areas, foreign capital had to tolerate conditions imposed by the government. For instance in the oil industry, the government enforced a production sharing contract system, which restricted the foreign partners to 15 per cent of the total output as a return for their investment, expertise and technology. In some areas of high technology, foreign capital was admitted only in joint venture with domestic capital. In manufacturing government allowed foreign firms to control production processes but explicitly reserved domestic distribution for Indonesian firms.

In the years following, foreign investment increased, but was always limited by political realities. There were cases of strong resentment against foreign capital on the issue of management control and technology transfer. Popular protests against the rise in Japanese investment occurred in 1974.[8] In response, government obliged new foreign ventures to reduce the foreign equity share to 80 per cent, and to reduce it further to 49 per cent within ten years.

In sum, state capital rose to a dominant position in the post-independence Indonesian economy. It deliberately suppressed the expansion of domestic capital which was independent of state capital. And it strictly controlled the inflow of foreign investment. After the crisis of the mid-1960s, the government was forced to become more flexible. The Soeharto regime maintained a dominant state sector as a counterweight to the possibility of outright Chinese dominance in the commercial and industrial sectors of the economy. But at the same time, the regime allowed selected business interests including Chinese interests to prosper,[9] usually in alliance with the government and state capital. Foreign investment was admitted to a larger but still limited extent within this overall framework of tight control and careful balancing of conflicting interests. State capital remained dominant, but it was obliged to allow more scope for domestic capital and foreign capital. The delicate *modus vivendi* worked out in this period survived through into the early 1980s.

Malaysia

As in Indonesia, the government which took over at independence used the strong state structure inherited from the colonial power to extend state capital and to limit the role of domestic capital controlled by ethnic Chinese. But the Malaysian case differed from that of Indonesia in one important respect: the relative size and power of the ethnic Chinese community. In Indonesia, the Chinese community was numerically small, and at the time of independence its business interests were still largely limited to domestic distribution. In Malaysia, the Chinese represented close to 40 per cent of the total population, and even at independence their business interests were extensive. The Malaysian Government's policies to develop the country on behalf of Bumiputra (i.e. indigenous Malay) interests have had to be more forceful and more controversial than in Indonesia. In this context, attitudes toward foreign capital inflow have been more complex.

At independence, the new Malaysian Government could appeal to Malay resentment against economic domination by foreigners, and against the economic prominence of the ethnic Chinese. There was no immediate large scale nationalization as in Indonesia, but the government did inherit the strong structure of state control established by the colonial power, which included state operation of public utilities, and expanded the activities to include telecommunications, electricity, and water works for the public at large. Then from the mid-1960s onwards, the role of state capital was substantially expanded. The Companies Act of 1965 permitted state enterprises to participate directly in trade, commerce, industry and finance.

Under the New Economic Policy (NEP) programme introduced in the early 1970s, the government extended the scope of state enterprises in order to increase the participation of the indigenous Malay population in business, and to reduce the Malaysian Chinese domination in trading, banking and most economic activities. In 1971, Bumiputras held 4.3 per cent of total equity in Malaysia, compared to 61.7 per cent held by foreigners and 34 per cent by other Malaysians, most of whom were ethnic Chinese.[10] Under the NEP the government planned to increase the equity share of the Bumiputras to at least 30 per cent by 1990.[11] The government also planned to increase the share of Bumiputras in total non-agricultural employment. Expansion of state capital was a major strategy for achieving both the equity and employment objectives.

New state enterprises were established in banking, steel, oil, airlines, heavy industry and automobiles. Several government banks were established to promote the development of Malay entrepreneurs. Government inaugurated ventures in co-operation with private Malay partners with the aim of eventually selling out the government share to Malays once the enterprises had proven profitable. Public enterprises were launched with trust agencies set up to hold shares on behalf of the Malay community. The Industrial Co-ordination Act (ICA) 1975 stipulated that 30 per cent of the equity and employment in enterprises of certain size (foreign or domestic) had to be Bumiputra owned.[12]

As far as the government and its Bumiputra allies were concerned, foreign investment was judged as good or bad depending on the extent to which it promoted the policy goals represented by the NEP. When the NEP was introduced in 1970, about 60 per cent of the Malaysian corporate sector was in the hands of foreign capital. Many British firms were bought out by the government or by the business groups associated with the major (Malay) political parties. This buying out offered a quick and relatively painless method to increase the equity share of Bumiputras in corporate capital. It did little to promote any further investment from the West.

By the early 1980s (1982–83), the Malaysian economy was in poor shape. The government achieved its aim of increasing Bumiputra ownership of capital, but it discouraged investment among Chinese entrepreneurs. The rate of growth of domestic investment (mostly from the Chinese) declined, and some Chinese capital fled from Malaysia.[13] At the same time, the new state enterprises established under the NEP tended to be inefficient. And Western foreign capital was discouraged by the prospect of another buy out in the future. The decline in oil prices in the early 1980s tipped the economy into a severe recession. The government and its allied groups then tried actively to promote foreign investment in ways which would support the NEP goals, and at the same time promote the overall growth of the economy. This was the background for launching the "Look East" policy in the early 1980s.

The "Look East" policy (1982) encouraged the inflow of Japanese and Korean capital to promote prosperity, and so strengthen the power of the state. The government structured incentives and imposed conditions to ensure that the new capital inflow would not serve as an ally of domestic Chinese capital. It allowed foreign companies to have 100 per cent ownership, thus tacitly discouraging joint ventures. It channelled much of the investment into free-trade zones which were relatively isolated from the rest of the economy. Here they contributed to employment and to the balance of payments without doing much to stimulate the growth of domestic enterprise. And the government established joint ventures between Japanese capital and state capital in such enterprises as the Proton car. Thus foreign capital was encouraged firstly to balance out the dominance of Chinese businesses, secondly in collaboration with state capital to crowd out local capital in certain sectors which had been Chinese dominated such as construction and automobiles (Lim and Pang 1988), and thirdly to provide high levels of employment.[14]

As in Indonesia, state capital rose to a dominant position in Malaysia. Initially it was opposed to competition from either domestic or foreign capital. In the mid-1980s, the government was forced to re-evaluate its attitude in order to sustain economic growth and to solve unemployment problems, but attempted still to control and manage the inflow of foreign investment in a way which would not undermine the dominant role of state capital.

Singapore

In both Indonesia and Malaysia, the dominant position of state capital tended to restrict the ambit of foreign capital. In Singapore, state capital was even more dominant. Yet in this case, it co-existed with foreign capital. Indeed the Singapore Government actively encouraged foreign capital inflow. The Singapore case illustrates a situation where the receptivity to foreign capital may have been due to the limited range of options open to a small country. Lack of local entrepreneurship and the limited size of the domestic market compelled the Singapore Government to adopt an export-oriented industrialization strategy with heavy reliance on foreign capital and technology.

In the 1960s, the Singapore economy relied on entrepôt trade and British military expenditure. The announcement of the British military withdrawal in 1967 threatened to exacerbate an unemployment situation which was already critical; unemployment was running at over 10 per cent.[15] At the same time, as was pointed out by Ng Chee Yuen (1989, p. 291),

... the people's expectations of the newly elected government
were high while the political situation was fluid. To legitimize
its position the new government had not only to be perceived
but also to be seen to actively promote economic development
that would better the livelihood of the electorate. This situation spawned a highly interventionist government.

Goh Keng Swee, the mastermind of economic policy at the time,
has described the situation thus:

> Taking an overall view of Singapore's economic policy, we can
> see how radically it differed from the laissez faire policies of
> the colonial era. These had led Singapore to a dead end, with
> little economic growth, massive unemployment, wretched
> housing, and inadequate education. We had to try a more ac-
> tivist and interventionist approach. Democratic socialist eco-
> nomic policies ranged from direct participation in industry to
> the supply of infrastructure facilities by statutory authorities,
> and to laying down clear guidelines to the private sector as to
> what they could and should do. (1976, p. 84)

This was the rationale for the Singapore Government to extend
the range of government enterprises far beyond the usual selection
of public utilities. One of the earliest ventures was into housing,
which ended with government emerging as the major player in the
housing market. By 1980, government managed 81 per cent of all
dwelling units, and planned to extend the proportion to 90 per cent
(Krause, Koh and Lee 1988, p. 118). To mobilize domestic savings
for this and other ventures, government introduced the Central
Provident Fund (CPF) as well as establishing the Post Office
Savings Bank which quickly expanded its activities in mass
consumer banking.

By 1986 there was a total of 608 government-linked companies
ranging from department stores to shipping yards (Ng 1988, p.
292). In some areas, such as airlines and shipping, government
remained the sole owner until recently. In others, government is a
major shareholder. The Development Bank of Singapore, for
instance, is 48 per cent government owned. In joint-venture
businesses the government has been active in steel, sugar, and
department stores (Yaohan, along with Japanese capital) and has
taken an equity share in a wide variety of other enterprises. The
government also invests overseas through the Government of
Singapore Investment Corporation.

The significance of state capital can be gauged from the number of workers in its employ: 58,000 in 1983 or 5 per cent of the total labour force (Krause, Koh and Lee 1988, p. 118). The size of the government sector as a whole is huge as can be seen from the government share of national saving. If the obligatory Central Provident Fund funds are included, on average public saving accounted for 46 per cent of gross national saving for the period 1974–85. For 1985 alone this share was 69.3 per cent (Koh 1988, p. 84).

Despite the extensive network of state capital in the economic life of Singapore, the government adopted a most positive policy stand towards foreign capital. From the beginning the government welcomed foreign capital almost unconditionally. The government actively identified foreign firms which were likely to find Singapore attractive, and invited their executives to Singapore to display the facilities available and to indicate the government's willingness to receive their investment. It imposed no restrictions on foreign equity participation except in certain industries like banking, newspapers and residential properties; no restrictions on remittances of earnings, or repatriation of capital; and relatively minor restrictions on the employment of suitably qualified foreign professionals and skilled workers.

The reasons behind the adoption of such a policy lay in the relative weakness of Singapore's domestic capital. As an entrepôt, Singapore possessed a business community more oriented towards trade and service activities rather than manufacturing. As a creation of colonial rule, Singapore had few sizeable businesses which were domestically owned. To promote industrialization, government reasoned it would be quicker and more efficient to invite foreign participation rather than nurture local capital out of its underdeveloped situation. As pointed out by Lim Chong Yah (1988, p. 252),

> Singapore was in a great hurry to industrialize, to restructure the economy away from the stagnating entrepôt trade and to combat large scale unemployment. But it did not have the wherewithal to unbundle the direct foreign investment package and to obtain the capital, technology and managerial and marketing expertise independently and efficiently. For such an infant industrial economy anxious to leap into international markets, a heavy dependence on MNCs with their well established marketing network was unavoidable.

Kunio Yoshihara has suggested another reason. Singapore's

economic growth had depended very much on the prosperity of
Malaysia and Indonesia, for which it acted as a service centre. By
inviting multinationals to use Singapore as an off-shore production
platform, Singapore lessened its dependence on its two neighbours.
Besides, the economic ties with powerful nations gave Singapore a
greater sense of security (1989, p. 118, 123).

Domestic private capital in Singapore was weak in all sectors.
In manufacturing, domestic capital was mainly confined to small
and medium enterprises, working as subcontractors to larger
enterprises. Only a few progressed with the help of the government
and links to foreign capital. In 1985, 65.7 per cent of manufactured
exports were produced by wholly foreign firms, 22.9 per cent by
part-foreign firms and only 11.4 per cent by wholly local firms.[16] In
construction, small-scale operations were dominated by domestic
capital, but the large-scale ones were dominated by foreign firms.

In sum, the Singapore Government followed a two-pronged
strategy: on the one hand developing state capital to an exceptional
degree, and on the other actively encouraging foreign capital to use
Singapore as a overseas base. The policy may have been forced on
the government by the weakness of the indigenous business community, but the policy also contrived to confirm that weakness.

Thailand

Unlike all the other member states of ASEAN, Thailand was never
formally colonized, and consequently never passed through the
stage of nationalism and independence. However, as a result of
unequal trade treaties with the West, the economy was under some
colonial influence from the mid-nineteenth century until around
1927.[17] In the other ASEAN states, the colonial period implanted a
relatively powerful state structure (bureaucracy, education, public
works), and the independence movement ended with this state
structure, relatively intact, taken over by a nationalist government
with a purposeful ideology of development and nation-building. It
was this process which created the foundations for the extension of
state capital. In Thailand during the same period, there was some
state-building activity in imitation of its colonized neighbours, but
nowhere near as advanced. And there was a surge of nationalism
in the decolonization period, but again it was played in a minor
key. The foundations for the extension of state capital were much
weaker in Thailand than in the other ASEAN states.

Like Indonesia and Malaysia, Thailand's business activity was dominated by ethnic Chinese, and this domination was resented by the Thai majority who were still mainly engaged in rice farming. From the 1930s to the 1950s, military-based governments espoused economic nationalism and attempted to transfer many Chinese-run businesses to state control. Many state enterprises were set up to replace the Chinese in rice trading, other distributive trades, manufacturing and banking.[18]

Thus Thailand began the 1950s with commitments to expand state capital and limit Chinese capital, very much along the lines of Indonesia and Malaysia. Yet by the end of the decade, these policies had been abandoned.

The relatively weak Thai state structure proved incapable of managing state capital on a large scale. In the 1960s and 1970s, most of the state enterprises created in the economic-nationalist era were sold back to private ownership. Only a handful, including tobacco and petroleum, remained under government control. Further extensions of state capital were limited to public utilities, and enterprises considered vital for defence or national development.

In the absence of the kind of strong religious barriers which exist in Indonesia and Malaysia, the ethnic Chinese in Thailand were able to achieve relatively successful social integration. Beginning in the 1950s, government and the ethnic Chinese business sector gradually worked out a way to coexist and co-operate. As in the other three countries studied, domestic capital in Thailand (mainly Chinese owned) was especially strong in distribution, in service industries, and in low-technology manufacturing. From the late 1950s onwards, with the help of limited government protection, Thai domestic capital grew in strength in these areas, and also expanded into manufacturing and export production.

In the 1960s and 1970s domestic capital developed in Thailand in agro-industries, consumer-goods industries, textiles and garments, jewellery, and automobile parts. Enterprises were not confined to producing goods for domestic markets, but branched out into successful export businesses in jewellery, garments, processed food, artificial flowers and other consumer goods. Several Thai-owned conglomerates emerged, such as Siam Cement, Charoen Pokphand, Mitr Phol and Saha Union. These enterprises started in the traditionally strong sectors such as commerce and construction and later diversified into various manufacturing ventures. Siam Cement began in construction but later developed

extensive manufacturing interests. Charoen Pokphand began in
distribution but grew into a multinational agro-industry. Mitr Phol
began as a sugar-cane grower and then branched out into sugar
manufacturing. Saha Union began in distribution but later
extended into manufacturing for the domestic market and export.

Among domestic capital, attitudes to foreign capital inflow
varied from sector to sector but were generally antithetical.
Especially in the areas of traditional strength (service, distribution, low-tech manufacture), domestic capital lobbied strongly for
foreign capital to be excluded. In subsectors where domestic capital
was strong and strongly organized, this pressure bore fruit. For
instance in banking, which is dominated by ten very powerful
families, the Thai Bankers Association was successful in opposing
the opening up of banking and insurance to foreign companies. In
the hotel trade, tourism and construction, domestic capital lobbied
government extensively and won some degree of favouritism versus foreign capital.

In manufacturing, the attitude to foreign capital was more
pragmatic. In subsectors where Thai domestic capital saw that the
only opportunity to gain access to the best technology lay through
collaboration with foreign capital, then foreign investment was
generally welcomed, but preferably in a joint-venture format which
could benefit domestic capital in some way.[19] In subsectors where
technology was easily available, foreign capital was viewed as a
threat and domestic capital lobbied hard for government assistance
to protect its interests. This was evident in areas such as textiles
and the manufacture of domestic appliances and automobile parts,
where domestic interests lobbied government to limit promotional
privileges to foreign firms.

The Thai Government's attitude to foreign capital, therefore,
was not influenced by the need to protect or extend the interest of
state capital. Rather its attitude was moulded by lobbying from
domestic capital interests, and by its own estimation of foreign
capital's contribution to state goals. In the 1960s, when domestic
capital in manufacturing was still relatively weak, the Thai Government gave in to pressure from the World Bank and the American
Government to provide a legal framework for the promotion of
foreign investment. As a result, the Investment Promotion Law
was passed in 1962. But significantly this law applied equally to
both domestic and foreign investment. It also required that a
majority share in any enterprise be Thai-owned (under a separate

agreement, this requirement was waived for American companies). These measures set the tone for the Thai Government's attitude to foreign capital through the 1960s and 1970s.

In sum, in the immediate post-war period Thailand appeared to be following the Malaysia-Indonesia pattern of building up a strong state sector. However, there proved to be no deep-seated popular support for this policy direction, and no adequate state structure to maintain it. As the role of state capital declined, domestic capital grew in importance. And policy-making with respect to foreign investment was to a large extent dictated by the demands of domestic capital exercised through lobbying of government. In this context, the Thai Government had no strong objections to foreign investment and provided a general framework for it to operate; but it was hardly enthusiastic about encouraging foreign investment, and tended to favour domestic capital interest by obliging foreign investors to enter into joint ventures.

Summary

In Indonesia, Malaysia and Thailand, the ethnic majority in the 1930s and the immediate post-war period used state power to reduce the role of Chinese entrepreneurs, by expanding state capital in public utilities, manufacturing, trading and other enterprises in competition with Chinese businesses. In Indonesia and Malaysia, the history of colonialism and independence created a strong state structure which provided a strong foundation for the extension of state capital. In addition in Malaysia, the policy of using state capital to limit the power of Chinese business under the NEP had widespread popular support. In both of these countries, state capital was well established in the 1960s, and expanded even further in the 1970s.

Thailand did not go through the same historical process. Without a strong state structure, state-sponsored economic nationalism faltered. In addition, ethnic rivalry petered out as the ethnic Chinese became socially assimilated. As a result incipient state capitalism was rolled back, and the government established a limited alliance with domestic capital.

In all four countries, domestic capital tended to perceive foreign capital as a competitor and lobbied government to offer some protection against foreign capital inflow or to help improve domestic capital's bargaining power. State capital also viewed foreign capital as a threat and only allowed very limited inflow. As a result of the military alliance with the United States, Thailand opened up somewhat to foreign capital from the early 1960s. And in all three countries, balance-of-payments difficulties in the late 1960s and early 1970s forced a re-evaluation of the role of foreign capital. In Malaysia, government tended to view foreign capital not only as a competitor to state capital, but also as a potential ally of the ethnic Chinese. In both Malaysia and Indonesia foreign capital was welcomed only insofar as it promoted the political and economic design of the state. Thailand began to admit more foreign capital but generally within the framework of joint ventures which offered benefits to domestic capital as well.

The Singapore case was very different. The ethnic factor was not relevant. The state opted to rely on foreign capital to promote export-oriented industrialization, while extending state capital widely in public utilities, banking, strategically important industries such as the airline, mass communication and shipping, and a host of other businesses which have some impact on public welfare. Access to foreign capital also gave Singapore greater economic and political security amidst the surrounding non-Chinese neighbours. Limited policy options due to lack of entrepreneurship and small domestic markets may have compelled the Singapore government to rely on foreign investment as a means to industrialize.

Up to the early 1980s, Singapore was the only one of the four countries to promote foreign investment with any degree of enthusiasm. For the other ASEAN countries, the crisis of the early 1980s created a dramatic change.

The fiscal and debt crisis of the 1980s

In the early 1980s economic growth rates in the United States and other major industrialized countries slowed down as they struggled to cope with the second oil price increase (Table 4.1). The United States and European countries faced chronic trade deficit problems and high unemployment. The European countries pursued restrictive fiscal and monetary policies to cope with inflation and rising trade deficits. Countries with high unemployment problems resorted to protectionism. Most countries abandoned the fixed exchange rate regime, and adopted some form of floating system, leading to greater fluctuations in the foreign exchange market. All

Table 4.1
Real growth rates: Selected countries
(In percentage)

	1960s	*1970s*	*1980s (1980–87)*
Japan	11.1	6.1	3.7
EC	4.6	2.9	1.6
United States	4.1	2.9	2.5
Canada	5.2	4.2	2.7
Australia	5.1	3.3	3.0
New Zealand	3.3	2.8	2.3
South Korea	8.6	9.1	8.8
Taiwan	9.6	8.3	7.2
Hong Kong	10.0	9.9	6.9
Singapore	9.2	9.1	5.8

SOURCES: MITI, International Trade Policy Bureau Asia-Pacific Trade and Development Study Group, Interim Report, *Toward New Asia-Pacific Co-operation Promotion of Multi-level Gradually Advancing Co-operation on a Consensus Basis* (June 1988).

of these reactions contributed to a decline in world trade. At about the same time over-supply of primary commodities depressed commodity prices in world markets. The economies of the ASEAN countries were severely affected. Growth rates slowed markedly after 1981, and slumped in 1985 and 1986 at the depth of the recession (Table 4.2).

In Singapore and Thailand during this period, the trade deficit widened. In Malaysia, the usual surplus was transformed into a small deficit. Indonesia reduced oil production in line with OPEC policy and saw its usually large trade balance severely reduced. The fall in oil prices after 1984 exacerbated the problems for both Malaysia and Indonesia. In all ASEAN countries, government revenue depended heavily on taxes levied on the import and export trade, so the trade recession affected government revenues. From 1981 to 1985, the share of government revenue in Gross Domestic Product (GDP) declined in Indonesia, remained constant in Malay-

Table 4.2
Real GNP growth rates
(In percentage)

	1960s	1970s	1980	1981	1982	1983	1984	1985	1986	1987	1988
Indonesia	3.9	7.6	9.6	8.0	4.5	2.9	4.5	1.9	3.2	3.6	5.0
Malaysia	6.5	7.8	.2	6.5	5.2	5.6	7.6	−1.0	1.2	5.2	7.4
Singapore	8.8	8.5	10.0	10.0	6.3	7.9	8.2	−1.8	1.2	8.8	11.9
Thailand	7.9	6.9	5.7	7.6	4.1	5.9	5.5	3.5	4.5	8.4	11.0

SOURCES: *World Development Report 1982*, official data from different countries.

Table 4.3
Central government revenue as percentage of GNP

	1981	1982	1983	1984	1985	1986
Indonesia	26.4	22.2	22.7	–	22.5	19.5
Malaysia	29.1	29.2	–	–	–	29.3
Singapore	28.0	28.5	30.8	–	28.7	27.0
Thailand	14.4	13.9	15.2	–	16.3	16.3

SOURCE: *World Development Report*, various issues.

sia, and Singapore and increased only slightly in Thailand (Table 4.3). In certain ASEAN countries in some years, government revenue was actually reduced in real terms.[20]

While interest rates were low in the 1970s, most ASEAN countries had borrowed abroad to cover their trade and budget deficits. Indonesia in particular had borrowed heavily. The private sectors of ASEAN states had also been tempted by low interest rates to borrow abroad to cover losses or increase capital. In the early 1980s, anti-inflationary macro-economic policies in the industrial countries led to a rapid rise in real interest rates, and ASEAN countries with large foreign debts were hit hard. The appreciation of the yen after 1985 exacerbated the problem, as debts denominated in yen suddenly multiplied in size. With around a third of its total debt denominated in yen, Indonesia suffered especially badly.

The combination of decelerating GDP growth, rising interest rates, and rising yen exchange rates increased both the overall debt burden and the debt service ratio. Malaysia's total external debt as a percentage of GDP rose to 62 per cent in 1985 and 77 per cent in 1986. In Indonesia external debt rose from 37 to 40 per cent of GDP over the same years. In Thailand, the absolute debt burden was less acute but the rise equally dramatic. From just 11 per cent of GDP in 1970, the debt burden jumped to 36 per cent by 1986.

The debt service ratio in Indonesia rose from 8 per cent in 1980 to 19.9 per cent in 1985. In Malaysia over the same period, the debt service ratio rose from 2.3 per cent to 22.3 per cent, and in Thailand from 3.4 per cent to 14.7 per cent. Only Singapore kept debt service at a manageable level. For the other three countries, by the

Table 4.4
Debt service ratio (public debt only, excluding private debt)
(Percentage of exports of goods and services)

	1970	1976	1980	1981	1982	1983	1984	1985
Indonesia	6.9	7.1	8.0	8.2	8.3	12.8	14.7	19.9
Malaysia	3.6	4.3	2.3	3.1	5.1	5.9	7.7	22.3
Singapore	0.6	0.8	1.1	0.8	0.8	1.3	1.0	2.4
Thailand	3.4	2.4	3.4	6.7	8.4	11.3	12.0	14.7

SOURCE: *World Development Report*, various years.

mid-1980s debt service had become a major problem (Table 4.4). It was also clear that the cause of the problem was the state sector, and particularly the inefficiency of state enterprises. In all three countries, over 70 per cent of the total external debt was public debt.[21]

The recession of the mid-1980s thus became a turning point for state capital. The policy of heavy reliance on state capital for development (especially in Indonesia and Malaysia) was in disfavour. It had created inefficient industries which had saddled the countries with heavy debt problems. To escape the immediate recession, countries needed a new source of capital. In these circumstances, government attitudes to foreign capital had to be revised. Where it had once been seen as a potential competitor to state capital, it now promised to serve as a tool to aid the state achieve its aim of continued economic growth and continued revenue generation.

Changes in foreign investment policies

The 1980s, and especially the period after 1985, saw changes in policies towards foreign direct investment in most of the ASEAN countries. All countries adopted some form of "privatization" and "deregulation" of the economy in favour of private domestic and foreign capital.

In Indonesia in 1974, the government had laid down the law that all foreign ventures must eventually be transformed into minority holdings. In 1986 this rule was relaxed and foreign firms were allowed to hold up to 95 per cent of the equity of a joint venture company for up to five years, on the condition that the increase in foreign equity enhanced the firm's export capacity. Also in 1974, the government had excluded all firms with any foreign equity participation from involvement in local distribution. In 1986 this was revised to allow joint venture firms with at least 75 per cent Indonesian equity to engage in domestic distribution. Joint-venture firms producing export products were also given access to low-interest export credit. In December 1987 foreigners were allowed to purchase shares in the Indonesian capital market. In late 1988, various import monopolies were abolished and the wholesaling, shipping and banking industries were reopened for foreign participation.[22] To improve the financial infrastructure and facilitate the operation of export firms, foreign banks were permitted to establish branches outside Jakarta.

The decline in oil prices and the debt crisis made it vital for the Indonesian government to increase exports. It was this economic factor which "provided the political will for substantial deregulation" (Pangestu and Habir 1989). Private domestic capital both from Chinese and Pribumi sources welcomed the change.

In Malaysia, 1986 saw several amendments to regulations affecting foreign investment. The government provided exemption from income and development tax for companies engaged in manufacturing new products or undertaking modernization, expansion or diversification, and modified the Bumiputra rule for foreign firms. It completely exempted foreign-owned firms from the requirements for Bumiputra shareholding and employment if they were medium-sized, or if they exported at least 80 per cent of their output. It also gave until 1990 for firms to apply for permission for 100 per cent foreign ownership as long as they exported at least 50 per cent of their output, employed at least 350 Malaysian workers, had a reasonable proportion of ethnic Malay workers, and did not compete against existing locally produced goods in the local market.

In Thailand, the government had set up a framework for promoting investment, including foreign investment, since the 1960s. But up to the 1980s the government had never felt an urgent need to promote foreign capital as a means to achieve economic growth. As a result, the operation of the investment promotion machinery for foreign firms was allowed to become bogged down by bureaucratic red tape. The foreign minority equity rule was strictly

enforced. Foreign investors regularly complained, and the World
Bank constantly agitated for reform. Nothing much resulted, however, until the recession of 1985/86 saddled Thailand with a huge
trade deficit and a high debt burden. Government then took a
renewed interest in foreign capital. Measures were taken to speed
up the procedures for granting promotion. The restrictions on foreign equity share were interpreted more flexibly. Firms which
exported 100 per cent of their products could now have 100 per cent
foreign ownership. Firms which exported at least 20 per cent of the
total output could automatically apply for export promotion
incentives such as exemption from business and export taxes on
export sales.

In sum, Singapore had positively encouraged foreign capital
inflow since the mid-1960s, but in the other three countries their
governments' attitudes to foreign capital had been influenced by
their desire to promote state capital and, in the case of Thailand, to
nurture domestic capital as well. The world recession, exchange
rate adjustments and oil price drop created a fiscal and debt crisis
which undermined the position of state capital. Deregulation, privatization and investment promotion policies were quickly imple-
mented to attract private capital, especially in export industries.

In all four countries, their governments reacted to the crisis of
the early 1980s by encouraging foreign capital inflow, rather than
by promoting domestic capital directly. There were several reasons
for this choice. First, domestic capital generally lacked the
technology needed to compete in international markets, and lacked
easy access to these markets. In both respects, foreign capital was
better equipped. Furthermore, in the case of Malaysia and to a
smaller extent Indonesia, a policy of promoting domestic capital
would involve high political costs which the governments were not
prepared to bear.

Domestic capital and the demand for foreign investment

While the debt problems of the mid-1980s had a direct impact on
the attitudes of ASEAN governments to the inflow of foreign
capital, the accompanying recession also influenced the attitude of
domestic capital in the countries concerned.

First, the difficulties experienced by government had an immediate impact on domestic capital in those countries where domestic

capital still depended greatly on links with government and with state capital. Decline in the number and profitability of government-awarded contracts, and a slow-down in joint public-private projects prompted major domestic capital interests to re-evaluate the prospects of working in joint venture with foreign capital.

This was particularly visible in Indonesia, the ASEAN member with the most predominant state capital sector, where some of the major business groups associated closely with the government increased the extent of their joint-venture business, particularly in co-operation with the Japanese. While such joint-venture business was not a new phenomenon, it increased dramatically in scale. The major ethnic Chinese business groups which enjoyed government favour led the trend. The Liem group established assembly projects with Hino, Suzuki and Mazda, and entered into housing development in joint venture with Marubeni.[23] The other leading ethnic Chinese group, Astra, established joint-venture projects in automobile assembly with Toyota, Daihatsu and Honda, and expanded into manufacture of automobile components in co-operation with Nippondenso, producing engines for cars with Daihatsu and Toyota, and manufacture of motor cycles with Honda. The group also entered into joint ventures with Japanese capital in distribution for Fuji Xerox, Toyota, Honda motor cycles, and Komatsu tractors. The Roda Mas group (Tan Siong Kie, alias Hanafi) is another leading Chinese business group which prospered in joint investment with Asahi Glass to manufacture glass and plastics, and in co-operation with Sumitomo (Steven 1988, p. 47). Major Pribumi groups were also active in joint projects with the Japanese, albeit on a lesser scale than the major ethnic Chinese combines. The Gobel group started joint investments with Matsushita and with Osaki Denki Kogyo. The Poleko group co-operated with Toray in synthetic textiles, with Mitsui in a plywood adhesive factory, and with Kao in a chemical factory. The Samudra group and the Mercu Buana group also invested jointly with Japanese capital (Steven 1988, p. 47).

Second, during the recession in the early 1980s, producers of consumer goods for the home markets faced stagnant or declining demand as the GNP growth rates slowed down or turned negative in some countries. At the same time, some producers of labour-intensive export products fared much better. This was particularly true of companies able to penetrate the market in Japan, which was far more buoyant than markets in the West. Some of these companies were joint venture firms whose foreign partners provided access to technology and external markets. Others were locally owned firms, producing labour-intensive products, for which the firms had clear comparative advantage (such as jewellery, artificial-flower making, animal feed, frozen chicken and canned seafood). The success of these export firms, some of which gained technology know-how and access to export markets through the collaboration of a foreign joint partner, created demonstration effects for other firms.

Two major factors defined the firms which were able to respond most readily to these demonstration effects. First, they often had a past history of co-operation with the Japanese, usually in assembly and distribution operations targeted at the domestic market. Such firms had already been through the learning process of working with the Japanese, and had their business contacts already in place. In many cases it was relatively simple to upgrade from an assembly or distribution operation to manufacture the same product range for both the domestic and export markets. In other cases, existing Japanese-domestic joint ventures branched out into new product lines in which the host country enjoyed a comparative advantage. And in other cases, domestic firms with existing Japanese joint ventures entered into additional ventures with totally separate Japanese groups.

Second, most of the firms which responded quickly to these demonstration effects were the larger and more developed business combines. They had the management resources to expand quickly for new ventures. And they were attractive partners for Japanese capital on account of their size and influence.

Both these factors were evident in Thailand. Many of the leading industrialists in Thailand had begun as trading firms selling Japanese and other foreign imports. Pornavalai reported that of 211 companies under the umbrella of 24 leading business groups in Thailand, 76 have had some business links with foreign firms in the past. Of the 76 companies, 61 have had business links with Japanese firms (Pornavalai 1988, p. 149).[24] Also, most of the large conglomerates in Thailand, with or without past experience in Japanese joint ventures, had been keen to enter into joint prospects since the mid-1980s. These ventures cover a wide range — real estate, tourism, automobile parts, electrical machinery, electronics, petrochemicals and various export products. They are attracted to Japanese collaboration because it offers technology, management know-how and access to Japanese and other markets. Since 1980, the country's largest industrial combine, the Siam Cement Group, has become increasingly involved in ventures with Japanese capital. Siam Cement co-operated with Kubota and Marubeni to manufacture diesel engines for agricultural machinery,[25] with Hino to manufacture automobile parts, with Toto to produce sanitary ware and sanitary porcelain, with Toshiba, Mitsubishi, Philips and a consortium of local firms to manufacture colour TV set tubes, and with Asahi Glass to manufacture bulb glass and colour TV sets. Recently Siam Cement and Mitsubishi agreed to set up a joint-venture trading company, Siam MC Co, to handle marketing in Eastern Europe. According to the Siam Cement President, the company benefited from the joint investment with Mitsubishi because it would be difficult for Siam Cement to enter non-traditional markets like Eastern Europe on its own. Since Mitsubishi already has marketing arms in Eastern Europe and around the world, teaming up with Mitsubishi offers new opportunities.[26]

The Siam Motors group is another large Thai business combine which has a long history of co-operation with Nissan in assembly and distribution of automobiles. It is now extending this joint venture to manufacture diesel and gasoline engines. Other companies in the Siam Motors Group are joining up with Komatsu to produce construction machinery, with Hitachi to make elevators, and with Daikin to make compression engines. Nissan has already announced plans to use Thailand as a base to supply markets in Taiwan, Malaysia, Bangladesh and Pakistan.

Another Thai firm, Charoen Pokphand, is an example of a firm which, without any previous Japanese relationship, entered into a joint venture with Japanese capital in the mid-1980s. Begun in 1921 as an import-export firm specializing in agro-products, Charoen Pokphand entered into a joint venture with an American firm in 1970 to import poultry breeding stock. In the 1970s and early 1980s, the firm grew into a diversified agro-product combine with operations in Indonesia, Taiwan, Malaysia, China and Thailand. In the mid-1980s, it embarked on a joint venture with Japanese capital to develop quality shrimp stock, and in the 1990s to invest jointly with a Japanese restaurant chain, Sky Lark.

Not all domestic capital was as keen to enter into Japanese joint ventures, or to welcome an inflow of Japanese investment. In several ASEAN states, domestic businesses which experienced no direct gain from the Japanese inflow expressed resentment. While large business combines have often been the most open to Japanese investments, smaller business interests have often been the most opposed.

Although the large Thai companies could benefit much from collaboration with Japanese capital this has not come about without tensions, especially in cases where joint investments entitled to promotional privileges come into direct conflict with smaller producers who are already supplying the local markets. These small and medium-sized firms which do not benefit directly continue to see Japanese investment as a threat. In particular, the government's decision to allow 100 per cent Japanese enterprises to enter into some new export businesses, and to release up to 20 per cent of their output into the local market, created resentment among competing domestic firms.

In Indonesia, Pribumi entrepreneurs continue to be suspicious of Japanese investment, but some have begun to consider joint ventures with the Japanese in export or in tourist businesses as a means to counter the decline in subcontracting from the government sector.[27]

In Singapore, the domestic retail trade has complained against competition from foreign companies and tried to lobby the government for assistance in excluding or limiting foreign competition. Also in Singapore, smaller manufacturing firms have lobbied for government support against foreign competition. In response, the government established a Small Enterprise Bureau within the Economic Development Board to help develop the small-scale sector, not in competition with foreign firms but in support of them through subcontracting arrangements.[28]

In Malaysia the question of support for or opposition to foreign investment has been coloured by investment regulations and the political environment. In general, major Bumiputra business groups have supported foreign investment. Even when allowed to operate as 100 per cent owned subsidiaries, several foreign firms prefer to take Bumiputra partners as a strategy to reduce business risks. Foreign alliances help emergent Bumiputra business groups grow stronger. At the same time, ethnic Chinese capital has found the new regulations discriminatory, particularly the 1986 modifications to the Industrial Co-ordination Act. Under certain conditions, foreign firms can be exempt from the rules requiring medium and large firms to have a certain level of Bumiputra shareholding and a certain level of Bumiputra employment but local firms owned by Chinese capital do not have the same exemption. In certain areas, ethnic Chinese firms find they now face increased competition from foreign firms, or from foreign-Bumiputra joint ventures.

The demand for new forms of investment

While domestic capital has tended to welcome foreign investment to a greater extent than in the past, there is also evidence that domestic capital has exerted some pressure to demand new forms of investment such as technology contracts rather than more traditional forms of equity investment.

Interviews with Thai and Indonesian firms engaged in alliances with Japanese firms showed that these firms were keen to unbundle the traditional investment package and gain access to technology without sacrificing equity share or management control. Several firms in Thailand and elsewhere had started out as more or less equal equity partners with Japanese firms and then progressively diluted the Japanese capital share in order to minimize foreign control.[29] The large local combines which have played the leading role as partners with Japanese firms in new wave ventures, often have the muscle to oblige the foreign partner either to accept a lower equity share, or to accept what amounts to a technology contract.[30] There are also examples of large local firms "shopping" for overseas partners.

In other words, the increasing importance of "new forms of investment" is at least to some extent demand-driven. This is perfectly rational. Comparative studies of firms operating under various joint-venture agreements in Korea, Indonesia and Thailand showed that firms with technology agreements and little or no foreign equity participation tended to show faster development of their technological capacity and ultimately a more rapid rate of growth and higher profitability than firms with more conventional foreign equity participation (United Nations 1987).

Summary

In the 1950s and early 1960s, when the ASEAN state governments were formulating their first phase of development policy, the demand from host countries for foreign investment was low everywhere except in Singapore. The fundamental weakness of domestic capital in Singapore, and the small scope of the home market, virtually obliged the government both to strengthen state capital and cultivate foreign capital. In Malaysia, Indonesia and Thailand, however, both the state and domestic capital were largely opposed to a large role being allowed for foreign capital.

For the governments of these three states, foreign investment in this period appeared to have two main disutilities. First, it would rival state capital which was the focus of national economic development policy. Second, it promised to be politically destabilizing. In Indonesia and Malaysia, the governments feared that foreign capital could ally with and strengthen the ethnic Chinese business groups which the government wished to control. In Thailand, a powerful role for foreign capital could run across the emerging alignment between government and domestic capital interests.

For domestic capital in this period, foreign capital was welcome only up to the point where it might threaten to overwhelm domestic capital interests. Where foreign capital threatened to overstep this rather low threshold, domestic capital lobbied for protection.

As a result, in this period the ASEAN states were not closed to foreign investment, but were not fully open either. Foreign investment was more or less confined to joint-venture projects in import-substitution assembly-type manufacturing operations.

Through the 1960s and 1970s, economic crises and changes of regime caused shifts in this basic policy in various countries at various times. However, this fundamental policy remained intact only until the early 1980s when an especially severe worldwide recession prompted a major revision.

By this time, there had been fundamental changes in the orientation of both governments and domestic capital groups in these three ASEAN states. From the viewpoint of governments, the need to protect and nurture state capital had virtually disappeared. State capital had largely failed to play a leading role in economic development and was now being blamed for causing a debt crisis. At the same time, governments now saw considerable utility in welcoming foreign capital in order to overcome debt and balance of payment difficulties, and to push the national economies out of recession. The potential political impact of increased foreign investment was still problematic, particularly for Malaysia and to a lesser extent for Indonesia. However, other positive factors outweighed this concern.

Meanwhile domestic capital had matured considerably and now felt much more confident in its ability to manage foreign investment to its own advantage than it had a decade before. Moreover, domestic capital was frustrated by the recession, convinced that the possibilities inherent in import-substitution industrialization were largely exhausted, and attracted by the potential which alliances with Japanese capital, technology and access to markets could offer in the area of manufacture for world export markets.

The firms which responded most readily to the potential advantages of joint ventures for export tended to be large firms which had the management capacity for expansion, and which often had a history of co-operation with overseas capital, particularly Japanese. In many cases, firms which had previously undertaken joint ventures in assembly and distribution now expanded into manufacture for both domestic and export markets. In other cases, major domestic business interests contracted a whole new series of ventures with overseas capital. These powerful domestic interests not only felt confident enough to manage the relationship with foreign capital to their own advantage, but in some cases also strong enough to demand that the relationship be constructed on their own terms. The pattern of joint activities has therefore become more diversified, including both joint ventures involving direct foreign investment in the conventional sense, and increasingly, the new forms of investment in which foreign equity participation and management control are substantially reduced.

Notes

1. See for example Allen (1973 *a,b,c*), Stoever (1982).
2. However, Chee (1989*a*, p. 362) does refer to this aspect briefly: "As developing countries strive to minimize the foreign exchange cost of acquiring foreign investment resources, while maximizing the contribution of those resources to domestic capital accumulation, they may seek to unbundle the traditional FDI 'package' (comprising financial capital, embodied or disembodied technology, management and, where relevant, access to world markets)."
3. Domestic capital refers to private investments by nationals of the country in question. State capital refers to enterprises or investment projects in which the government has an equity participation.

Investment projects carried out by private individuals who have high positions in the bureaucracy or who have connections with high level bureaucrats, sometimes referred to as bureaucratic capital, are not considered state capital unless equity participation by the government is involved. State capital is also domestic, but in this study the phrase "domestic capital" is reserved for private investment by nationals of the country in question to avoid confusion. Foreign capital refers to enterprises or projects that have equity participation by foreign companies. For our purposes, the precise magnitude of the share of each type of capital in the case of a joint venture is not an issue as we are not concerned so much with the quantitative as the qualitative aspect of different types of capital.

4. The writer benefited greatly from the theoretical discussion on the role of the state in Indonesia in Chapter 4 of Robison (1986), and from a discussion with Lysa Hong of the Department of History, National University of Singapore.

5. Information in this section is from the following works: Gale (1985), Heng Pek Koon (1988), Jesudason (1989), Krause, Koh and Lee (1988), Ng (1989), Pangestu and Habir (1989), Pipatsereetham (1983), Pornavalai (1989), Robison (1986), Suehiro (1988), Tan Chwee Huat (1974), Thee and Yoshihara (1987), Toh Kin Woon (1989), Yoshihara (1988).

6. When Soeharto came into power after 1965, Indonesia's new leaders agreed to end the nationalist policies of state-led industrialization under Soekarno and to promote private investment in the consumer goods and agricultural sectors. They also agreed to draft a new foreign investment law which gave better incentives to foreign capital. See Robison (1988) p. 61. And following the anti-Japanese riots of 1974, the government had to introduce several measures to protect domestic capital, including a requirement that foreigners must take indigenous joint-venture partners. The period between 1977 and 1985 also saw a decline in foreign capital investment in the non-oil sector, although the oil sector was still dominated by foreign investment. See Robison (1988) p. 64. Thus, although Soeharto's government showed a more favourable attitude towards foreign investment than Soekarno's government, nationalist and radical forces opposed to foreign capital circumscribed the Soeharto Government's policies towards foreign investment The government could not appear to be openly supportive of foreign investment, even though it relied on foreign capital and technology for the operation of the oil industry, and on foreign assistance and loans for development funds. It is in this sense that I described the the attitude of the Soeharto Government towards foreign capital as "lukewarm". The fiscal crisis, brought on by the decline in government revenue and increased public debt following the fall in oil prices after 1984, provided legitimacy for the government to be more open to foreign investment. This policy, still objected to by certain nationalist

elements, was supported by bureaucrats who could benefit from the open policy, and by a powerful segment of domestic capital including many who had been adversely affected by the decline in government expenditure (e.g. contractors who had relied on contract work from the government), and many who now saw joint investment with foreign capital as a new source of profitable ventures.

7. Investment Law and Regulations, Investment Co-ordination Board, Indonesia (undated, probably 1987).

8. The protest was much more of an expression of resentment against the Soeharto government. It broke out as an anti-Japanese investment demonstration. Nevertheless it indicated a public resentment against foreign investment, and the visibility of Japanese investment in particular.

9. Indeed Robison (1986) had argued that under Soeharto's rule Chinese capital prospered and provoked resentment among some Pribumi capitalists.

10. Mid-Term Review of the Third Malaysia Plan 1976–1980, Tables 3 to 5, p. 49.

11. By 1985 Malays had achieved ownership of 17.8 per cent of total capital, with other Malaysians holding 56.7 per cent and foreigners holding 25.5 per cent (Mid-Term Review of the Third Malaysia Plan 1976–1980, p. 9 and 22).

12. In the early years of its introduction, the rule applied to manufacturing firms with share capital of M$250,000 and above. In 1986 the government raised the size of share capital of companies having to meet the ICA provision to M$2.5 and above. Companies which employ 75 full-time workers and above are also required to follow the rule.

13. See further details in Chapter 5 of Jesudason (1989). He also discussed the ways in which the Chinese gravitated their new investment towards commercial projects which gave quick returns like property development rather than high risk and longer term investment in manufacturing.

14. See also Jesudason (1989), especially Chapter 6, for an excellent discussion of the attitudes of state élites towards the roles of multinationals in Malaysian economy and society.

15. Augustine H.H. Tan (1984, p. 35) reported that the unemployment rate was 13.5 per cent in 1959.

16. Report on the Census of Industrial Production 1985. Department of Statistics, Singapore, January 1987, as reported in Lim and Associates (1988), p. 250.

17. The Bowring Treaty signed with Great Britain in 1855 and subsequently with other Western countries allowed Thailand to impose only 3 per cent import duties. The Treaty contained clauses which prohibited Thailand from imposing taxes other than those agreed in the Treaty. Thailand recouped some financial autonomy in 1927, and

fully in 1936.

18. The attempt to replace Chinese in business in the 1930s and 1940s also had a political motive, i.e. to prevent Chinese from sending remittances back to China. See Pornavalai (1989) pp. 30–37.

19. Indeed many Thai business groups which began as importers/ distributors have benefited from collaboration with Japanese capital. Nine out of the 24 major industrial groups in Thailand in the 1980s started off as importers of Japanese goods. Later when the Thai government pursued import-substitution industrialization with high tariffs, these distributors were among the first who went into joint venture with Japanese manufacturers to establish factories to assemble imported components and parts of the previously imported consumer goods. The nine major industrial groups had altogether 211 companies. Of these, 76 had some association with Japanese capital, either as joint venture or technological agreements. Their success as modern industrialists was aided by the joint investment and partnership with Japanese capital. Siam Cement did not have close association with Japanese capital from the beginning, but has recently gone into joint venture with Japanese capital for technological reasons. See Pornavalai (1989) pp. 139–50. Other groups such as Charoen Pokphand benefited from a licensing agreement with American capital and later moved into joint investment with Japanese capital as well.

20. In Indonesia since the mid-1970s, the government's domestic revenue has been met primarily from taxes on oil company profits because of its inability to generate revenue from other potential sources of public revenue. Revenue in nominal terms declined from Rp 19,253 billion in 1985/86 to Rp 16,141 billion in 1986/87, largely as a result of the decline in oil prices. The revenue shortfall caused a decline in development expenditure even in nominal terms. The total development expenditure in billions of Rupiahs for 1985/86, 1986/87, 1987/88, and 1988/89 were as follows: 10.873, 8,332, 7,757 and 8,897. The decline in development expenditure had implications for the government's stability, and the government was forced to become dependent on foreign borrowing to meet its budgetary objectives. The information is from the Economic Intelligence Unit, Country Profile Indonesia 1988–89, pp. 58–61.

21. The ratio of public to total external debt in 1985 was 87.4 per cent in Indonesia, 77.1 per cent in Malaysia and 74.4 per cent in Thailand. Data are from the *World Development Report 1987*.

22. *Business Times*, 22 November 1988.

23. Associated with the Liem Group are the Kencana Group, the Bank of Central Asia group and the Lippon group. The Liem group is closely connected to the Soeharto family and other leading members of the Chinese community. The head of the group, Liem Sioe Liong (alias Soedono Salim), engaged in trading and military supplies in the

independence struggles (1945–49) during which time he built up his connections with senior military officials and Soeharto. The groups also had joint projects with other foreign investors. Much of the business of the group is dependent on state concessions and investment projects. In areas which require technical and industrial expertise such as automobile assembly, the group has tended to rely on foreign capital. See Steven (1988) pp. 43–48.

24. Among the leading business groups in Thailand are Siam Motors, the Metro group, Sahapatanapibul, Saha Union, Pothiratanangkun, Boon Sung, and the Cathay Trust groups.

25. Siam Cement has received constant technology transfer from its Japanese partners. In its joint-venture project with Kubota to manufacture diesel engines, for example, the Japanese partner provided expertise and technology to both the joint-venture company and its fifty-plus subcontractors, with the result that 80 per cent of the engine parts are produced in Thailand. "New SCG Joint Ventures Reflect Export Campaign", *Bangkok Post Weekly Review*, 13 August 1989, p. 18.

26. Ibid.

27. Data from interviews conducted with business groups in Jakarta in 1988.

28. Data from interviews conducted in Singapore in 1988. In a study of foreign investment in Malaysia, Thailand, Singapore and Taiwan, Lim Y.C. Linda and Pang Eng Fong (1989) cited examples of local producers in Singapore which benefited from collaboration with Japanese capital, such as Softech, a consortium of seven local companies which have teamed up with United Japan Inc., a Japanese software house, to market their products in Japan. They cited other examples of successful collaboration between local and other multinational firms. They concluded that the Singapore government's encouragement of multinationals in the electronic industry has not worked against the interest of local producers.

29. In Thailand this occurred in the Suzuki motor group, and in the Sukree textiles group. See Yoshihara (1988) p. 31.

30. Many of the recent ventures between Thailand's Siam Cement conglomerate and Japanese firms amount to modified technology contracts.

5

Conclusions and prospects

The nature of the new wave

The new wave of Japanese direct investment in manufacturing in ASEAN since 1985 differs from the old wave in both scale and character. Japanese direct investment in ASEAN over the three years from 1985 to 1987 totalled over US$3.3 billion compared to an accumulated total of US$12.5 billion over the previous three decades.[1] Manufacturing investment in the old wave focused mostly on resource-based and import-substitution industries, producing for the domestic markets of host countries. Ventures usually involved the assembly of components and parts imported from Japan. The old wave increased exports of semi-raw materials, parts, components and machinery from Japan. The investment was mostly joint venture with local partners. Big Sogo Shosha played an important role in matching and organizing the joint ventures, and sometimes were directly involved in the local production jointly with the Japanese manufacturers and local partners.

The new wave is significantly more export-oriented.[2] The Japanese firms involved are both final manufacturers and their subcontractors, including a large number of small and medium-sized enterprises. They prefer 100 per cent ownership to joint ventures, particularly in competitive export-oriented sectors such as electronics components, electrical machinery, food processing and automobile parts. As Japanese overseas investment is becoming more export-oriented, the new wave leads to an increase in exports of manufactures from ASEAN to Japan and to third countries.[3] Several Japanese firms are developing complex production networks spanning several countries, resulting in increased intra-firm trade among Japanese subsidiaries, and between subsidiaries and the headquarters. There is also evidence of increased local sourcing by Japanese subsidiaries or joint-venture firms, thereby increasing backward linkages with local subcontractors and material producers. Japanese firms are also developing new forms of investment, usually involving contractual sales of innovative technology and management to local producers in return for minority equity share.

The analysis of Japanese overseas investment

Foreign direct investment is a distinct form of capital movement because investors have direct control over management and production in their overseas operations. Early attempts to analyse foreign direct investment as a form of international capital movement within the framework of the theory of international trade proved to be inadequate because they simply failed to match the empirical evidence.

Within modern writings on the theory of foreign direct investment, three prominent approaches are represented by: Western economists interested in the behaviour of large multinational firms, especially those of American origin; Japanese economists who are concerned to explain the motivation of Japanese direct investment during the mid-1960s and 1970s, and writers from host countries who are concerned about the benefits and costs of foreign direct investment to the host economy and society.

Western approaches

Western economists attempted to explain overseas investment within micro-economic analysis, using two different approaches.

The first was the industrial organization approach pioneered by Hymer and further elaborated by Caves, Kindleberger and others. This approach argued that for a firm to engage successfully in overseas investment it must possess firm-specific advantages unavailable to rival local firms. These advantages may be production or management know-how, marketing technique or access to specific materials. By establishing and directly controlling overseas operations, the firm could realize the full returns on these specific advantages in many different markets. Alternative strategies for marketing firm-specific advantages, such as technology sale or licensing arrangements, would yield lower returns. But the existence of firm-specific advantages alone was not sufficient to explain the profitability of overseas investment by multinational firms. Imperfections in the markets created the conditions which ensure that the firm could exploit its specific advantages through discriminatory pricing. Some writers in this group stressed that firms invested overseas, especially in locations where production costs are lower than in the home market, in order to pre-empt competitors. There was a monopolistic element involved in the motivations.

A second group of Western economists, often known as transaction theorists, focused their attention on the ability of multinational firms to minimize the costs of firm organization overseas by internalizing costs involved in the transaction of their activities. The reduction of transaction costs gave these firms advantages over local competitors and increased the attractiveness of overseas direct investment.

Japanese approaches

In the 1970s, Japanese investment in ASEAN increased rapidly and prompted some adverse political reactions. Subsequently, Japanese economists became interested in the analysis of foreign investment. Kojima rejected the micro-economic approach favoured by Western economists and analysed Japanese investment flows within a framework of comparative advantage. He argued that Japanese direct investment in Southeast Asia in the 1960s and 1970s occurred in industries in which Japan had been losing comparative advantage due largely to high labour costs. According to trade theory, such investment flows promote the international division of labour, increase trade between the two countries, and offer welfare gains for both parties. Host countries benefit from increased capital investment and increased employment. Kojima distinguished this type of direct investment as being characteristically Japanese, and contrasted it with foreign direct investment induced by imperfections in the markets which he suggested was characteristically Western.

Ozawa also wrote on foreign investment within the frame of comparative advantage but argued that scarcity of natural resources in Japan was the key factor pushing firms to invest overseas. Ozawa added that Japanese firms would have been too weak to invest overseas on their own, and allocated an important role to the assistance which the Japanese Government provided to firms venturing overseas.

Other Japanese writers in the period more or less followed the comparative advantage framework. Some acknowledged a need to integrate decision-making at the firm level into the analysis. And some were sceptical of the welfare implications of Kojima's hypothesis. Critics pointed out that Kojima's analysis simply reflected a particular stage of the economic development of Japan, and predicted (correctly as it turned out) that as Japan reached the same level of industrial maturity as the United States, the pattern of Japanese direct investment would become more like that of the United States. In other words the monopolistic character of American foreign investment was not unique.

Host country approaches

Economists from ASEAN host countries tended to see no substantial difference between the motivations of American and Japanese firms. In their view, both were monopolistic. Both were concerned to conserve and exploit their specific advantages, hence the low level of technological transfer. Several studies from host countries showed that Japanese firms were more restrictive than American or European firms in transferring technology and skills.

All of these approaches concentrated on the supply side. They analysed the motivations of the investing firms or the comparative advantages of the investing countries. They considered the host countries in terms of the investment climate, the state of political stability, and certain specific policies such as tariffs and investment promotion.

The supply side of the new wave

In the past decade, the Japanese economy experienced rapid structural change: from primary to secondary industry; then from light manufacturing, labour-intensive products to capital-intensive, heavy and chemical industries, and recently a shift to knowledge-intensive industries, and information technology. These shifts caused rapid rises in labour productivity followed by intense upward pressure on wage rates. In this process of rapid structural change, Japan gained comparative advantage in many high-tech, knowledge-intensive areas, but at the same time lost comparative advantage as a site for many of the production processes which had been the mainstay of the economy in the immediately preceding period.

The consequences of these structural changes were postponed for some time by two factors: wage restraint, and the artificially low exchange rate for the yen. When these two factors were removed, the impact was dramatic. Rising wages and rising yen-denominated prices suddenly made it uneconomic for many firms to retain certain production processes in Japan. To continue to grow and remain dominant in the market worldwide, firms had to upgrade production technology or relocate these processes to cheaper production locations overseas. For many firms, the most attractive or most feasible option was relocation.

Japanese firms could relocate all or part of their production processes and still remain competitive because of their firm-specific advantages of various kinds. These advantages included vertical linkages to the high-tech processes in which Japan held comparative advantage; accumulated skills in management, production and marketing; innovations in firm organization which minimized the costs of transnational operations; and marketing properties such as brand names. Japanese firms invested overseas because such investment enabled them to realize more profitability (short or long-term) than through licensing the technology or brand name.

At the same time, Japanese firms increasingly experimented with other methods of realizing profit from these firm-specific advantages. These methods, sometimes referred to as new forms of investment, included technology contracts, long-term licensing arrangements, brand name franchising and co-operative production arrangements.

The demand side of the new wave

There is a demand side to the foreign investment equation. Host countries can exhibit a greater or lesser demand for foreign investment with clear and palpable consequences for potential investors. Where demand is high, entry costs and profitability thresholds can be significantly lowered, thereby resulting in the reduction of transaction costs for foreign firms.

There are two main factors in the demand function: the attitudes and strategies of government, and the attitudes and strategies of domestic capital. Other factors could also be included, particularly the role of labour. But in the circumstances of ASEAN states in the 1980s, these two factors predominate. For domestic capital the utilities of foreign direct investment lie in the profitability of joint enterprises, the potential access to technology, management know-how, marketing assets and export opportunities. At the same time there are potential disutilities arising from increased competition in the same product markets; increased competition for scarce resources of manpower, infrastructure and natural resources, and political alliances between government and overseas investors to the detriment of domestic capital.

For the government the utilities of foreign investment are important in relation to its three main roles: as a manager of macro-economic policies, as an investor, and as a political manager.

As an executor of macro-economic management policies, the government sees the utility of foreign direct investment in the context of "national economic development". Does it contribute to GNP rate of growth? Does it help the balance of payments? Does it enhance the level of technology or labour skills?

As an investor, governments assess the potential impact of foreign capital on state-owned economic interest. All ASEAN governments invest in public utilities and in various types of state enterprise. In sectors where government investment dominates, the government may try to exclude foreign investors. Or in other circumstances, it may welcome participation in cases where government enterprises need technology from foreign sources.

As a political manager, the government views foreign investment as a force in power politics. The government must assess the likely impact of foreign investment on the political stability of the state, and on the balance of political forces which sustains the government itself in power.

In the mid-1980s, several factors conspired to increase the demand for foreign investment in the ASEAN states. The configuration of factors differed from country to country.

In the period from the 1950s to the early 1980s, most ASEAN governments, with the notable exception of Singapore, had been lukewarm towards foreign investment for two main reasons. First, they expanded state capital significantly in the 1950s and 1960s and tended to view foreign capital as a potential competitor to state capital. Second, they feared that foreign capital would strengthen sections of domestic capital which the government did not favour. However, by the early 1980s, the importance of these two factors had generally diminished. State capital had failed to dynamize economic development and was in retreat in most states. And ASEAN governments felt more confident of their abilities to manage the politico-economic impact of foreign capital inflow. At the same time, the recession of the early 1980s made foreign capital an attractive option for alleviating the debt burden and regenerating economic growth. As a result of these forces, in 1985–88 ASEAN governments were prepared to revise rules and promotional incentives to encourage investment inflow.[4]

The attitude of domestic capital towards foreign investment was also favourably affected by the recession of the early 1980s. Many of the avenues of opportunity open to domestic capital in the 1970s appeared to be closing off. First, as state capital retreated, so too did the opportunities for government contracts and joint public-private ventures. Second, the recession in Western markets blunted export possibilities. And third, opportunities for import-substitution investment seemed to be exhausted. Against such a background, the examples of firms that penetrated Japanese and other overseas export markets with the assistance of technology and marketing advantages gained from joint ventures with Japanese capital created a powerful demonstration effect. In many countries major business interests, particularly those with experience of co-operation with Japanese capital in earlier distribution and import-substitution ventures, were keen to expand into more complex manufacturing ventures, often with an export orientation, in conjunction with Japanese technology and perhaps also equity participation.

In sum, four main factors lay behind the increase of Japanese investment into ASEAN in the late 1980s. First, structural changes in the Japanese economy dramatically altered the pattern of comparative advantage and forced many production processes to relocate outside Japan. Second, Japanese firms increasingly commanded specific advantages in terms of technology, management skills, organizational assets and marketing properties (including access to the increasingly important Japanese market for manufactured imports), that enabled them to realize profits through investment in a variety of overseas markets. Third, against a background of recession and exhaustion of import-substitution growth, large-scale domestic capital in ASEAN perceived that Japanese capital and technology would deliver advantages both directly through joint-venture operations[5] and indirectly through a general stimulus to the domestic economy. Fourth, ASEAN governments perceived that Japanese capital inflow would help relieve the debt burden and regenerate economic growth without seriously disturbing delicate politico-economic balances which sustained these governments in power.

The future prospects of the new wave

Identifying these four major factors provides us with a framework for assessing the likely course of the new wave into the future. In what ways will these supply and demand forces alter in the near future?

The trend of change in Japan's comparative advantage is likely to continue in the foreseeable future. The structural change in Japan is not yet complete. Costs of labour, land and other inputs are still rising and are likely to go on rising for many years yet. As they do, even medium-tech firms will start to face declining comparative advantage if they remain located in Japan. Increasingly, firms placed further up the technological ladder will face pressures to relocate to cheaper production environments. More firms with specific advantages will go out into the world trying to realize an optimum rent from their accumulated knowledge and innovative technology.

Japanese firms are also likely to accumulate more specific advantages and be increasingly better placed to exercise monopolistic control in overseas markets. They will also become more global in their outlook, more like American multinational firms. We can expect the outflow of Japanese capital to continue, both because of continuing changes in comparative advantage and because of the dynamism propelling the growth of oligopolistic firms. Based on forecasts made by the Japan Economic Research Centre (JERC), Japanese investment of around US$14 billion will flow into ASEAN between 1988 and 2000.

These forecasts extrapolate from current trends which are largely favourable. However there are factors which have the potential to limit, inhibit or even reverse the flow of Japanese investment funds into ASEAN.

First, improvements in automation technology could provoke a reverse flow back to Japan. In certain production processes, including high quality textile and garment manufacturing, this reversal is already taking place (Velasco 1988). Second, Japanese investment may be diverted away from ASEAN in favour of other markets such as the United States and Europe on the one hand, and lower-cost producers such as China or South Asia on the other hand.[6] Third, Japan has already expressed fears about the "hollowing out" of its industrial base if industry is allowed to relocate overseas freely, and the government may undertake measures to restrict the flow.

All these are possibilities. But they are also conditional. First, even though automation and other technological upgrading may induce flowback in certain industries, there will still be Japanese manufacturing capital which will be attracted to overseas sites which offer comparative advantages. As the processes being squeezed out of Japan move up the technological scale, the factors creating comparative advantage will move beyond supplies of land, labour and other basic inputs. These processes will require a more sophisticated production environment including educated and trainable labour, technical expertise, provision of high-level infrastructure, and good support services. If ASEAN countries are able to offer these facilities, then they will continue to attract Japanese capital.

Second, while it is true that Japanese policy-makers have become concerned about the hollowing out of Japan's industrial base, it will become less and less easy for the policy-makers to control the trend. As Japanese firms become more powerful and more multinational, they will respond more to the logic of their own profit interests, and will be far less closely tied to the domestic economy. Thus on the supply side, the pressures to sustain the flow of Japanese investment are likely to remain strong. The demand side is more complex.

The current enthusiasm on the part of domestic capital in ASEAN to welcome foreign investment may prove fragile and short-lived. To begin with, there are already signs of division between mainly large-scale firms which are well-placed to profit from joint ventures and tie-ups on the one hand, and smaller scale firms which fear greater competition and crowding out on the other. While the smaller firms currently wield less political influence and tend to be ignored, this situation may change.

Next, in countries where the government is attempting to manage the relationship of foreign capital with local firms, excluded local interests tend to perceive the results as discriminatory. This may become an issue in Malaysia, where government guides foreign capital into ventures with *Bumiputra* rather than ethnic Chinese capital.

Finally, even among firms which gain immediate benefits from Japanese capital inflow, their attitude may change rather rapidly over time, for two main reasons. First, they will increasingly discover the potential in other sources of overseas capital, such as the Asian NICs, Europe and the United States. Second, as domestic capitalists themselves become stronger and more experienced, the "quality" of Japanese investment will increasingly become more important than the volume. Third, domestic capital will want to have more control over the operation of the joint enterprise. Especially in Singapore and Thailand, domestic capital can be expected to lobby for more non-traditional direct investments, such as licensing agreements, technology contracts and management tie-ups, as opposed to direct equity participation from overseas partners.

The governments' enthusiasm for foreign investment may also prove fragile. ASEAN governments' relatively sudden conversion in favour of foreign investment took place against a background of economic recession and a looming debt crisis. As the ASEAN economies boom and the debt problem recedes, some of the utilities of foreign investment as far as the governments are concerned will become less evident. At the same time, there are risks that foreign investment will provoke political problems, either arising out of business competitiveness, or out of a more general widening social division. The benefits of economic growth sparked by foreign investment tend to be concentrated at one end of the socio-economic scale — in the relatively rich cities rather than the relatively poor countryside, and among the more skilled, more monied and better educated sections of urban society rather than the masses. Most ASEAN countries already have relatively skewed income distributions. In Malaysia and Thailand for instance, the gini coefficients for income distribution are around 0.5. The initial inflow of Japanese investment in 1987–88 coincided with booms in commodity prices and in service industries, especially tourism, and these have to some extent spread prosperity more widely and balanced out the potentially divisive trends of growth based on export-oriented foreign investment. But this benign situation may not continue. If the three large ASEAN economies covered in our study face a new economic crisis due to a dramatic decline in commodity prices or stagnation of manufactured export growth, the problems of income inequality could flare into a political issue. And the public could come to see over-dependence on Japanese investment as a major cause of recession and economic difficulties.

Prospects for the impact on domestic capital

In previous analyses of the impact of foreign investment, the key issue for economists in host countries was the transfer of technology, skills and know-how. As noted earlier, it is premature to make any empirical assessment of the extent of such technology and skill transfer in the new wave of Japanese investment. However, this theoretical analysis leads to some important perspectives.

On the negative side, this analysis of the evolution of the overseas Japanese firm suggests that these firms will become increasingly aware of the profits available from the exploitation of their specific advantages, including their command of technology, skill and know-how. To that extent, they are likely to wish to conserve these assets and limit their transfer to host country firms.

However, there are other features of the new wave of investment which have strongly countervailing and much more positive effects. First, the logic of multinationalization will oblige Japanese firms to "domesticate" overseas operations more than in the past. Moves to establish operational headquarters, R&D facilities, and more decentralized decision-making are already evident.

Second, competitive forces will compel Japanese firms to use local subcontractors, to train local employees, and to provide technical assistance to local suppliers in order to remain competitive in world markets *vis-à-vis* competitors from Asian NICs.[7] The

JETRO survey of Japanese subsidiaries in ASEAN in 1988 indicated a greater degree of local sourcing and backward linkages with local firms than was evident in the past. The survey also indicated that local sourcing was more common in the countries with a more sophisticated industrial base, indicating the importance of upgrading the capabilities of support industries in order to gain greater value from overseas investment.

Third, domestic firms will copy and learn from Japanese venture firms located in their markets. This happened in the era of import substitution, when local firms in several countries successfully emulated the operations of foreign ventures. There is no reason to suppose that this trend will not continue into the era of export-oriented manufacture.

The fact that skills, technology and know-how will likely be transferred to local producers during the new wave leads to another important aspect of the impact of the new wave: domestic capital will be strengthened. Through the process of learning by doing, and through increasing exposure to the modern management and marketing techniques of Japanese firms, domestic capital in ASEAN will have the opportunity to accumulate management skills and upgrade technical capability relatively quickly.[8]

Some implications for policy-making

This framework of analysis indicates several areas of importance for ASEAN policy-makers interested in sustaining the flow of Japanese investment and in gaining maximum value from it.

First, the supply conditions pushing investment out from Japan are not static but dynamic. The features which made ASEAN an attractive site for Japanese firms moving out in the mid-1980s may not be demanded by a later wave. In particular, as the processes being squeezed out move up the technological scale, so will the firms be looking overseas for a more sophisticated production environment. The countries which most successfully construct such a production environment — including suitably skilled labour, adequate infrastructure, and good support industries — will benefit most.

Second, if governments wish to sustain the inflow of Japanese investment, they will need to pay close attention to the political repercussions of policies which attempt to manage the relationship between overseas and domestic capital. They will also need to support domestic firms in their attempts to upgrade the quality of their participation in joint-venture partnerships. Here ASEAN governments could learn from the example of Korea, where the government imposed progressively more stringent conditions on the nature of foreign investment deals with the aim of progressively increasing the benefits derived by domestic partners.

Third, ASEAN governments must pay special attention to the issue of distribution. For a variety of reasons, export-oriented growth tends to widen economic inequalities. And widening economic inequality threatens to disrupt the political environment which favours investment inflow. It will be important for governments to pursue policies which equip the more vulnerable sections of society with the capacity both to contribute to economic growth and share in its benefits. Such policies include measures to allocate land rights and deter land concentration, programmes to facilitate agricultural diversification, and investments in upgrading the education and skill levels of the labour force.

Fourth, the inflow of Japanese investment offers many opportunities for local firms to benefit, with largely beneficial long-term implications for the economy as a whole. However, the ability of domestic firms to develop in the era of the new wave will depend to a large extent on the assistance they receive from government. In the medium-term, this factor will become an important differentiator of the relative success of each country in building up its own industrial capacity.

Government can assist local firms in the areas of research and development, and skill upgrading. ASEAN countries will best benefit from Japanese direct investment if their manpower has a high capacity to absorb technology transfer, and this will require an upgrading of the educational levels of the labour force, as well as a step up in R&D assistance for local firms.

Government can assist local firms to become more competitive in the world market, by exposing them to outside competition rather than protecting them with high tariffs. As Hal Hill concluded, the impact of foreign investment on domestic capital is more positive in an environment of free trade rather than a situation of protection (Hill 1988).

One key issue which governments will have to manage concerns ownership. During the old wave, most Japanese direct investment was in the form of joint ventures with local capital. Government regulations forced a local equity majority in most countries, and the Japanese usually complied because local collaboration could reduce the risk elements involved in operating in alien situations. In the era of the new wave, small and medium firms in export-oriented industries from Japan would like to retain 100 per cent foreign ownership. Host countries have generally complied with their wishes for fear that continued stringent equity rules could turn away Japanese investment at the time when the economies needed an injection of outside capital. This open policy has the advantage that it does not discourage firms with special specific advantages, thus allowing host countries to benefit from the variety of modern expertise that Japanese firms command. But 100 per cent foreign firms producing for exports by assembling components and parts imported from their own subsidiaries from all over the region, tend to resort to transfer pricing among themselves to circumvent government regulations and taxation.[9] To achieve better overall welfare effects, and to achieve the maximum possible transfer of technology and skills, governments should force foreign capital into joint-venture arrangements.

Final comment

In sum, the key forces behind the new wave of foreign investment are the structural change in the Japanese economy, the evolution of the Japanese multinational, the perception on the part of host governments that foreign capital can regenerate sluggish growth, and the perception on the part of host-country domestic capital that Japanese capital inflow provides necessary access to technology, skills and markets. In the medium-term future, these factors will continue to operate, but their intensity will differ from country to country depending on the will and skill of governments to manage the impact of Japanese investment for maximum effect.

Notes

1. Japanese Ministry of Finance figures as reported in Toru Nakakita, "The Globalisation of Japanese Firms and Its Influence on Japan's Trade and Developing Countries", *The Developing Economies* 26 no 4. (1988): 308.

2. As are the parallel waves of new foreign investment from Taiwan, Korea and Hong Kong.

3. To be precise, it is not the new wave which increases exports. Rather, it is the underlying economic fundamentals — comparative wage levels, exchange rates, and government policies. And it is not only *Japanese* investment which is attracted to export industries; Korean, Taiwanese, Hong Kong and Singaporean capital are attracted to the same opportunities. However, Japanese investment plays a leading role for several reasons — notably the importance of the Japanese market as a destination for these exports.

4. Together with the increased inflow of Japanese investment to be expected in the future, ASEAN governments also expect an increase in overseas development aid from the Japanese Government. It is a well-known fact that the Japanese Government utilizes its aid programme to improve the profitability of Japanese investors.

5. Or through technology contracts and other new forms of investment.

6. Besides, ASEAN can expect a growing investment inflow from Korea, Taiwan and Hong Kong.

7. However, M.K. Chng has pointed out that, "A number of foreign firms also show preference in sourcing from subcontracting firms of their own nationality for a number of reasons other than the poorer performance of indigenous subcontractors ... The Japanese firms rationalize this carry-over as co-prosperity for the user and subcontracting industries. The cultural background, work attitudes and styles of firms of the same nationality also make symbiosis more conducive. For instance, a Japanese subcontractor would empathize and attempt to oblige an urgent order of another Japanese firm more readily than perhaps an indigenous which may have greater difficulties motivating workers to do overtime work." In M.K. Chng et al. *Technology and Skills in Singapore* (Singapore: Institute of Southeast Asian Studies, 1986), p. 78.

8. At the same time, the trend of decline in the importance of state capital is likely to continue. And this will have political implications. The liberalization policies and pressure for the contraction of the state sector after 1985 will permit the domestic capital sector and the middle class to grow and expand rather rapidly.

9. Of course transfer pricing is a tactic available to joint-venture firms as well. But 100 per cent or majority foreign firms almost certainly find it easier to practise.

References

Akrasanee, N. and J. Ajanant. "Manufacturing Protection in Thailand, Issues and Empirical Studies". In *The Political Economy of Manufacturing Protection: Experiences of ASEAN and Australia,* edited by Findlay, C. and R. Garnaut. Sydney, Boston and London: Allen & Unwin, 1986.

Allen, Thomas W. *Direct Investment of Japanese Enterprises in Southeast Asia.* Study No. 1. The Economic Cooperation Centre for Asian and Pacific Region, 1973*a*.

____. *Direct Investment of United States Enterprises in Southeast Asia.* Study No. 2. The Economic Cooperation Centre for Asian and Pacific Region, 1973*b*.

____. *Direct Investment of European Enterprises in Southeast Asia.* Study No. 3. The Economic Cooperation Centre for Asian and Pacific Region, 1973*c*.

____. *The ASEAN Report.* Vol. 1. Hong Kong: Asian Wall Street Journal, 1979.

Ariff, M. and H. Hill. *Export Oriented Industrialisation: The ASEAN Experience.* Sydney: Allen & Unwin, 1985.

Arndt, H.W. "Professor Kojima on the Macroeconomics of Foreign Direct Investment", *Hitotsubashi Journal of Economics* 15, no. 1 (June 1974).

Bix, Herbert P. "Japan's New Vulnerability", *Monthly Review* 34, no. 7 (December 1982).

Bergsten, C. Fred, Thomas Horst, and Theodore H. Moran. *American Multinationals and American Interests.* Washington D.C.: The Brookings Institution, 1987.

Buckley, P.J. and M.C. Casson. *The Future of the Multinational Enterprise*. London: Macmillan, 1976.

Casson, Mark, ed. *The Growth of International Business*. London: Allen & Unwin, 1983.

_____. *Firm and the Market*. Cambridge Mass.: MIT Press, 1987.

Caves, R.E. "International Corporation: The Industrial Economics of Foreign Investment", *Economica* 38 (February 1971).

_____. "Causes of Direct Investment: Foreign Firms' Shares in Canadian and United Kingdom Manufacturing Industries", *Review of Economics and Statistics* 56 (1974).

_____. *Multinational Enterprise and Economic Analysis*. Cambridge: At the University Press, 1982.

Chee Peng Lim and P.P. Lee. *Japanese Direct Investment in Malaysia*. Tokyo: Institute of Developing Economies, 1979.

Chee Peng Lim. "ASEAN Co-operation in Industry: Looking Back and Looking Forward". In *ASEAN at the Crossroads: Obstacles, Options and Opportunities in Economic Co-operation*, edited by Noordin Sopiee, Chew Lay See, and Lim Siang Jin. Kuala Lumpur: Institute of Strategic and International Studies, 1987.

Chee Peng Lim. "The Changing Role of Transnational Corporations in the Asian-Pacific Region". In *Global Adjustment and the Future of Asian-Pacific Economy*, edited by M. Shinohara and Fu-Chen Lo. Tokyo and Kuala Lumpur: Institute of Developing Economies, and Asian and Pacific Development Centre, 1989a.

_____. "Japan's Foreign Direct Investment in ASEAN: Changes and Implications". Paper presented at the International Conference on "Japan, the United States and ASEAN in the Next Decade", organized by the Institute of East Asian Studies, Thammasat University, Bangkok, 25–46 March 1989b.

Chen, E.K.Y. *Multinational Corporations, Technology and Employment*. London: Macmillan, 1983.

_____. "Technological Change in the Electronics Industry and Implications for the Asian Pacific". Paper presented at the 17th Pacific Trade and Development Conference, Bali, Indonesia, 20–23 July 1988.

_____. "The Changing Role of the Asian NICs in the Asian-Pacific Region Towards the Year 2000". In *Global Adjustment and the*

Future of Asian-Pacific Economy, edited by M. Shinohara and Fu-Chen Lo. Tokyo and Kuala Lumpur: Institute of Developing Economies, and Asian and Pacific Development Centre, 1989.

Chng, M.K. "ASEAN Economic Co-operation: The Current Status". In *Southeast Asian Affairs 1985*. Singapore: Institute of Southeast Asian Studies, 1985.

____. "A Comparative Study of the Industrialisation Experiences of the ASEAN Countries". Centre for Asian Studies, University of Hong Kong, 1989.

____ and R. Hirono, eds. *ASEAN-Japan Industrial Co-operation, An Overview*. Singapore: Institute of Southeast Asian Studies, 1984.

Chng, M.K. et al. *Technology and Skills in Singapore*. Singapore: Institute of Southeast Asian Studies, 1986.

____, Linda Low, and Toh Mun Heng. Industrial Restructuring in Singapore. Singapore: Chopmen Publishers, 1988.

Chinwanno, C. and S. Tambunlertchai. "Japanese Investment in Thailand and Its Prospects in the 1980s". In *ASEAN-Japan Relations: Investment*, edited by Sueo Sekiguchi. Singapore: Institute of Southeast Asian Studies, 1983.

Clapham, C. *Third World Politics: An Introduction*. Madison: University of Wisconsin Press, 1985.

Coase, R.H. "The Nature of the Firm", *Economica* 4 (November 1937).

Dicken, P. "The Changing Geography of Japanese Foreign Direct Investment in Manufacturing Industry: A Global Perspective", *Environment and Planning A* 20, no. 5 (May 1988).

Doner, R.F. "Weak State - Strong Country? The Thai Automobile Case", *Third World Quarterly* 10, no. 4 (October 1988)

Dorodjatun Kuntjoro-Jakti et al. "Japanese Investment in Indonesia". In *ASEAN-Japan Relations: Investment*, edited by Sueo Sekiguchi. Singapore: Institute of Southeast Asian Studies, 1983.

Dunning, J.H. *American Investment in British Manufacturing Industry*. London: Allen & Unwin, 1958.

____. "The Determinants of International Production", *Oxford Economic Papers* 25 (1973).

_____. ed. *Economic Analysis and the Multinational Enterprise*. London: Allen & Unwin, 1974.

_____. *International Production and the Multinational Enterprise*. London: George Allen & Unwin, 1981.

_____. *Multinational Enterprises, Economic Structure and International Competitiveness*. Chichester, New York: John Wiley & Sons, 1985.

Economic Development Institute of the World Bank and the National Centre for Development Studies, Australian National University. *Managing Trade and Industry Reform in Asia: The Role of Policy Research*. Background Papers. Canberra: Australian National University, 1989.

Economic Planning Agency, Japan. *Economic Survey of Japan 1986–87* (Economic White Paper). Tokyo, 1987.

Euh Yoon-Dae and Sang H. Min. "Foreign Direct Investment from Developing Countries, the Case of Korean Firms". *The Developing Economies*. XXIV, no. 2 (June 1986).

Evans, Peter. *Dependent Development: The Alliance of Multinational, State, and Local Capital in Brazil*. Princeton: At the University Press, 1979.

Fong Chan Onn. "The role of MNCs in Foreign Investment in ASEAN". Paper presented at the 13th Annual Conference of the Federation of ASEAN Economic Associations, Penang, Malaysia, 17–19 November 1988.

Fukuma, Tsukasa. "Global Wheels/Nissan Motor Co.", *Journal of Japanese Trade and Industry* 6, no. 4 (1987).

Gale, B. *Politics and Business: A Study of Multi-Purpose Holdings Berhad*. Petaling Jaya: Eastern University Press, 1985.

Galenson, W. ed. *Foreign Trade and Investment: Economic Development in Newly Industrialising Asian Countries*. Madison: University of Wisconsin Press, 1985.

Goldsbrough, D. "Foreign Direct Investment in Developing Countries: Trends, Policy Issues and Prospects", *Finance and Development* 22, no. 1 (March 1985).

Goh Keng Swee. "A Socialist Economy that Works". In *Socialism That Works: The Singapore Way,* edited by C.V. Devan Nair. Singapore: Federal Publications, 1976.

Gross M. "Foreign Direct Investment in ASEAN: Its Sources and Structure", *Asian Economics* 61 (June 1987).

Hattori, Tamio. "Technology Transfer and Management Systems", *The Developing Economies* 24, no. 4 (December 1986).

Heng Pek Koon. *Chinese Politics in Malaysia.* Oxford University Press, 1988.

Hennart, Jean-Francois. *A Theory of Multinational Enterprise.* Ann Arbor: University of Michigan Press, 1982.

Hiemenz, U. "Foreign Direct Investment and Industrialisation in ASEAN Countries", *Weltwirtschaftliches Archiv* 123, no. 1 (1987).

Hewison, K.J. "The State and Capitalist Development in Thailand". In *South East Asia, Essays in Political Economy of Structural Change*, edited by R.A. Higgott and R. Robison. London: Routledge & Kegan Paul, 1985.

Hill, H. and B. Johns. "The Role of Direct Foreign Investment in Developing East Asian Countries", *Weltwirtschaftliches Archiv* 121, no. 2 (1985).

Hill, H. *Foreign Investment and Industrialisation in Indonesia.* Singapore: Oxford University Press, 1988.

Horst, H.T. *A Home Abroad: A Study of Domestic and Foreign Operation of the American Food Processing Industry.* Cambridge: Ballinger Publishing Co., 1978.

Hufbauer, G.C. "The Multinational Corporation and Direct Investment". In *International Trade and Finance: Frontier for Research*, edited by P.B. Kenen. Cambridge: At the University Press, 1975.

Hymer, S.H. *The International Operations of National Firm: A Study of Direct Investment.* Cambridge, Mass.: MIT Press, 1976.

Imai, Ken'ichi. "Technological Change in the Information Industry and Implications for the Pacific Region". Paper presented at the 17th Pacific Trade and Development Conference, Bali, Indonesia, 20–23 July 1988.

Ingavata, P. "Privatisation in Thailand: Slow Progress Amidst Much Opposition", *ASEAN Economic Bulletin* 5, no. 3 (March 1989).

Ishii, Hayato. "Direct Overseas Investment Chokai and Corporate Principles/Matsushita Electric Industrial Co.", *Journal of Japanese Trade and Industry* 6, no. 4 (1987).

Islam, I. and C. Kirkpatrick. "Export-led Development, Labour Market Conditions and the Distribution of Income: The Case of Singapore", *Cambridge Journal of Economics* 10, no. 2 (1986).

James, W.E., S. Naya, and G.M. Meier. *Asian Development Economic Success and Policy Lessons*. Madison: International Center for Economic Growth, University of Wisconsin Press, 1987.

Japan Economic Research Centre. *Five-Year Economic Forecast 1988–1992*. Tokyo (February 1988).

Jesudason, J.V. *Ethnicity and the Economy: The State, Chinese Business, and the Multinationals in Malaysia*. Singapore: Oxford University Press, 1989.

JETRO. *Report of a Survey on Conditions of Japanese Affiliates in ASEAN*. In Japanese. Tokyo (March 1988).

Kindleberger, C.P. *American Business Abroad: Six Lectures on Direct Investment*. New Haven: Yale University Press, 1969.

_____. *International Economics*. Homewood, Ill.: Richard D. Irwin, 1973.

Kitamura Hiroshi. "Foreign Aid and Investment: New Challenges to Japan", *The Developing Economies* X, no. 4 (December 1972).

Knickerbocker, F.T. *Oligopolistic Reaction and Multinational Enterprise*. Cambridge, Mass.: Harvard University Press, 1974.

Koh Ai Tee. "Saving, Investment and Entrepreneurship". In L.B. Krause, Koh Ai Tee, and Lee Tsao Yuan, *The Singapore Economy Reconsidered*. Singapore: Institute of Southeast Asian Studies, 1988.

Koike, Kazuo. "Skill Formation System: A Thai-Japan Comparison", *Journal of the Japanese and International Economics* (1987).

Kojima, Kiyoshi. "Reorganisation of North-South Trade: Japan's Foreign Economic Policy for the 1970s", *Hitotsubashi Journal of Economics* (February 1973a).

_____. "A Macroeconomic Approach to Foreign Direct Investment", *Hitotsubashi Journal of Economics* (June 1973b).

____. *Direct Foreign Investment: A Japanese Model of Multinational Business Operations*. London: Croom Helm, 1978.

Komoda, Fumio. "Japanese Studies on Technology Transfer to Developing Countries: A Survey", *The Developing Economies* XXIV, no 4. (December 1986).

Koo Young Boh. "The Role of Direct Foreign Investment in Korea's Recent Economic Growth". In *Foreign Trade and Investment: Economic Development in the Newly Industrialising Asian Countries*, edited by W. Galenson. Madison: The University of Wisconsin Press, 1985.

Krause, L.B., Koh Ai Tee, and Lee Tsao Yuan. *The Singapore Economy Reconsidered*. Singapore: Institute of Southeast Asian Studies, 1988.

Kunasirin, Busaba. "Economic Fluctuations and Its Consequences for Small- and Medium-scale Industries". Working Paper No. 3001, Faculty of Economics, Chulalongkorn University, Bangkok, 1987.

Lee Chung H. "On Japanese Macroeconomic Theories of Direct Foreign Investment", *Economic Development and Cultural Change* 32, no. 4 (July 1984).

Lim, Joseph Y. "Japanese Investment in the Philippines: The Experience During the Eighties". Paper presented at the FAIR Conference, Tokyo, 20–22 April 1988.

Lim, X.C. Linda and Pang Eng Fong. "Foreign Investment, Industrial Restructuring and Changing Comparative Advantage: The Experiences of Malaysia, Thailand, Singapore and Taiwan". A Report prepared for the OECD, Paris, June 1988.

Lim Chong Yah and Associates. *Policy Options for the Singapore Economy*. Singapore: McGraw-Hill Book Company, 1988.

____ and Soon Teck Wong. "Foreign Investment and Economic Development in Singapore: A Policy Oriented Approach". Paper presented at the first conference organized by the Foundation for Advanced Information and Research of Japan (FAIR), Export-Import Bank of Japan, Tokyo, 20–22 April 1988.

Lim Joo-Jock et al. *Foreign Investment in Singapore: Economic and Socio-Political Ramifications*. Singapore: Institute of Southeast Asian Studies, 1977.

Mahathir, M. "Keynote Address". In *ASEAN at the Crossroads: Obstacles, Options and Opportunities in Economic Co-operation*, edited by Noordin Sopiee, Chew Lay See, and Lim Siang Jin. Kuala Lumpur: Institute of Strategic and International Studies, 1987.

McClintock, B. "Recent Theories of Direct Foreign Investment: An Institutionalist Perspective", *Journal of Economic Issues* XXII, no. 2 (June 1988).

Mid-Term Review of the Third Malaysian Plan 1976–1980. Kuala Lumpur: Malaysian Government Press.

Malaysian Industrial Development Authority. *Malaysia: Investment in the Manufacturing Sector, Policies, Incentives and Procedures*. Kuala Lumpur: MIDA, 1988.

Michalopoulos, Constantine. "Private Direct Investment, Finance and Development", *Asian Development* 3, no. 2 (1985).

Mirza, Hafiz. *Multinationals and the Growth of the Singapore Economy*. London and Sydney: Croom Helm, 1986.

MITI. *Toward New Asia-Pacific Cooperation: Promotion of Multilevel, Gradually Advancing Cooperation on a Consensus Basis*. Interim Report by the Asia-Pacific Trade and Development Study Group. Tokyo, 1988*a*.

_____. *Small Business in Japan 1988* (White Paper on Small and Medium Enterprises in Japan. Tokyo, 1988*b*.

_____. *White Paper on International Trade*. Tokyo, 1988*c*.

Mori, Takeshi, ed. *Japan's Overseas Investment*. Proceedings of the Symposium held from 10–13 November 1975 at the Institute of Developing Economies. Tokyo: 1976.

Nakakita, Toru. "The Globalisation of Japanese Firms and Its Influence on Japan's Trade and Developing Countries", *The Developing Economies* 26, no. 4 (December 1988).

Nathabhol et al. *Technology and Skills in Thailand*. Singapore: Institute of Southeast Asian Studies, 1987.

Naya, Seiji and Narongchai Akrasanee. *Thai-Japanese Economic Relations: Trade and Investment*. Study no. 9. Bangkok: The Economic Cooperation Centre for the Asian and Pacific Region, 1974.

National Economic and Social Development Board, Thailand, United Nations Centre on Transnational Corporations, United Nations Development Programme. "Foreign Direct Investment in Thailand". Bangkok, August 1986.

Ng, C.Y., R. Hirono, and Robert Y. Siy, Jr. *Technology and Skills in ASEAN: An Overview*. Singapore: Institute of Southeast Asian Studies, 1986.

Ng, C.Y., R. Hirono, and Narongchai Akrasanee, eds. *Industrial Restructuring in ASEAN and Japan: An Overview*. Singapore: Institute of Southeast Asian Studies, 1987.

Ng, C.Y. "Privatization in Singapore: Development with Control", *ASEAN Economic Bulletin* 5, no. 3 (March 1989).

Ohlin, Bertil. *Interregional and International Trade*. Cambridge, Mass.: Harvard University Press, 1933.

Ohmae, Ken'ichi. "Global Economics: Multinationals", *Japan Times*, 7 December 1988.

Oman, Charles. *New Form of International Investment in Developing Countries*. Paris: OECD, 1984.

Osman-Rani, H., Toh Kin Woon, and Anwar Ali. *Technology and Skills in Malaysia*. Singapore: Institute of Southeast Asian Studies, 1986.

Ozawa, Terutomo. *Multinationalism, Japanese Style: The Political Economy of Outward Dependency*. Princeton, N.J.: Princeton University Press, 1979.

____. "Japan". In *Multinational Enterprises, Economic Structure and International Competitiveness*, edited by J.H. Dunning. Chichester, New York: John Wiley & Sons, 1985.

Pangestu, Mari and Ahmad D. Habir. "Trends and Prospects in Privatization and Deregulation in Indonesia", *ASEAN Economic Bulletin* 5, no. 3 (March 1989).

Panglaykim, J. *Japanese Direct Investment in ASEAN: The Indonesian Experience*. Singapore: Maruzen Asia, 1983.

Phongpaichit, Pasuk. "Decision-Making on Overseas Direct Investment by Japanese Small and Medium Industries in ASEAN and the Asian NICs", *ASEAN Economic Bulletin* 4, no. 3 (March 1988).

Pipatsereetham, Krikkiat. *An Analysis of the Ownership of Large Conglomerates in Thailand*. In Thai. Bangkok: Thammasat University Press, 1983.

Pornavalai, Suvinai. *Japanese Enterprises and The Strategy of Thailand to be NIC*. Bangkok: Faculty of Economics, Thammasat University, 1989.

Rana, Pradumna, B. "Recent Trends and Issues on Foreign Direct Investment in Asian and Pacific Developing Countries". Asian Development Bank Economic Staff Paper No. 41, March 1988.

Robison, R. *The Rise of Capital*. Sydney: Allen and Unwin, 1986.

____. "Authoritarian States, Capital-Owning Classes, and the Politics of Newly Industrialising Countries: The Case of Indonesia", *World Politics* XLI, no. 1 (October 1988).

Santikarn, M. *Technology Transfer: A Case Study*. Singapore: Singapore University Press, 1981.

Sekiguchi, Sueo, ed. *Japanese Direct Investment*. Montclair: Allanheld, Osmun and Co., for the Atlantic Institute for International Affairs, 1979.

____ and Lawrence B. Krause. "Direct Foreign Investment in ASEAN by Japan and the United States". In *ASEAN in a Changing Pacific and World Economy*, edited by Ross Garnaut. Canberra: Australian National University Press, 1980.

____, ed. *ASEAN-Japan Relations: Investment*. Singapore: Institute of Southeast Asian Studies, 1983.

Shinohara, Miyohei and Fu-Chen Lo. *Global Adjustment and the Future of Asian-Pacific Economy*. Tokyo and Kuala Lumpur: Institute of Developing Economies, Asian and Pacific Development Centre, 1989.

Sopiee, Noordin, Chew Lay See and Lim Siang Jin, eds. *ASEAN at the Crossroads: Obstacles, Options and Opportunities in Economic Co-operation*. Kuala Lumpur: Institute of Strategic and International Studies, 1987.

Southard, F.A. *American Industry in Europe*. Boston, 1931.

Steven, Rob. "Japanese Foreign Direct Investment in Southeast Asia: from ASEAN to JASEAN", *Bulletin of Concerned Asian Scholars* 20, no. 4 (October–December 1988).

Stoever, William A. "Endowments, Priorities, and Policies: An Analytical Scheme for the Formulation of Developing Country Policy Toward Foreign Investment", *Columbian Journal of World Business* (Fall 1982).

Suehiro, Akira. *Capital Accumulation in Thailand 1855–1985*. Tokyo: The Centre for East Asian Cultural Studies, 1989.

Suzuki, Yoshio. *Money and Banking in Contemporary Japan*. Translated by John G. Greenwood. New Haven: Yale University Press, 1980.

Tan Chwee Huat. "State Enterprise System and Economic development in Singapore." Ph.D. thesis, University of Wisconsin, 1974.

Tan H.H. Augustine. "Changing Pattern of Singapore's Foreign Trade and Investment Since 1960". In *Singapore: 25 Years of Development*, edited by You Poh Seng and Lim Chong Yah. Singapore: Nan Yang Xing Zhou Lianhe Zaobao, 1984.

Tambunlertchai, S. and M. Krongkaew. "Recent Trends of Japanese Direct Investment in Thailand". Paper presented at the FAIR Conference, Tokyo, 20–22 April 1988.

Taylor, Michael and Nigel Thrift. *Multinationals and the Restructuring of the World Economy*. London: Croom Helm, 1986.

Thee K.W. "Japanese Direct Investment in Indonesian Manufacturing", *Bulletin of Indonesian Economic Studies* 20, no. 2 (August 1984a).

————. "Industrial and Foreign Investment Policy in Indonesia Since 1967", *Southeast Asian Studies* 25, no. 3 (December 1987).

———— and Kunio Yoshihara. "Foreign and Domestic Capital in Indonesian Industrialization", *Tonan Ajia Kenkyu* (March 1987).

Thorn, S. *The Rising Yen*. Singapore: Institute of Southeast Asian Studies, 1988.

Toh Kin Woon. "Privatization in Malaysia: Restructuring or Efficiency", *ASEAN Economic Bulletin* 5, no. 3 (March 1989).

Torii, Takashi. "Development of Electronic Industry in Malaysia With Special Reference to Japanese Firms". In *Industrial Development in Asia and Trade Conflict*, edited by Toshiaki Hayashi. Tokyo: Institute of Developing Economies, 1988.

Tran Van Tho. "Japan Technology Transfer and the Division of Labour in the Asian Pacific Region". Paper presented to the International Symposium on "Toward Restructuring the Division of Labour in the Asian Pacific Region: Economic Relations of Japan, China, NICs and ASEAN in the Year 2000", Pattaya, Thailand, 2–3 November 1987.

Tsukasaki, Seichi. "Japanese Direct Investment Abroad", *Journal of Japanese Trade and Industry* 6, no. 4 (1987).

Tsurumi, Yoshi. *Multinational Management: Business Strategy and Government Policy*. Cambridge, Mass.: Ballinger Publishing Company, 1984.

United Nations. *Technology Transfer Under Alternative Arrangements with Transnational Corporations*. Bangkok: ESCAP/ UNTCT Joint Unit on Transnational Corporations, Economic and Social Commission for Asia and the Pacific, 1987.

Velasco, Emmanuel T. "Technological Change in Textile Industry and Implications for the Pacific Region". Paper presented at the 17th Pacific Trade and Development Conference in Nusa Dua, Bali, Indonesia, July 1988.

Vernon, Raymond. "International Investment and International Trade in the Product Cycle", *Quarterly Journal of Economics* 80, no. 2 (May 1966).

____. "Government-MNC Relations". In *Proceedings of a Conference on MNCs and ASEAN: Development in the 1980s*, 7–10 September 1980, Singapore, edited by Arun Senkuttuvan. Singapore: Institute of Southeast Asian Studies, 1981.

Von Kirchbach, F. "Transnational Corporations in the ASEAN Region: A Survey of Major Issues", *Economic Bulletin for Asia and the Pacific* 33, no. 1 (1982).

Watanabe, T. "An Analysis of International Interdependence among the Asian NICs, the ASEAN Nations and Japan", *The Developing Economies* 18, no. 4 (1980).

Watanabe, S. "Inter-Sectoral Linkages in Japanese Industries: A Historical Perspective". In *Technology, Marketing and Industrialisation: Linkages Between Large and Small Enterprises*, edited by S. Watanabe. Delhi: Macmillan for the International Labour Organisation, 1983.

Watanabe, T. and H. Kajiwara. "Pacific Manufactured Trade and Japan's Option", *The Developing Economies* 21, no. 4 (December 1983).

Wells, L.T. Jr. *The Product Life Cycle and International Trade*. Mass.: Harvard University Press, 1972.

Westphal, L.E. et al. "Foreign Influences on Korean Industrial Development", *Oxford Bulletin of Economics and Statistics* 41, no. 4 (1979).

Williamson, Oliver. "Market and Hierarchies: Some Elementary Considerations", *American Economic Review* 63 (May 1973).

Wong Chin Yeow. "The Japanese Economy: Adjusting to New Realities". Paper presented at the Fifth US-ASEAN Conference, organized by Institute of East Asian Studies, University of California, Berkeley and Singapore Institute of International Affairs, 11–16 June 1989, Singapore.

Yoshihara, Kunio. *Foreign Investment and Domestic Response: A Study of Singapore's Industrialisation*. Singapore, Kuala Lumpur, Hong Kong: Eastern University Press, 1976.

____. *Japanese Investment in Southeast Asia*. Monographs of the Centre of Southeast Asian Studies. Honolulu: The University Press of Hawaii, 1978.

____. *The Rise of Ersatz Capitalism in Southeast Asia*. Singapore: Oxford University Press, 1988.

The Author

Pasuk Phongpaichit is Associate Professor in Economics, and
Director of the Centre for Political Economy Studies, Chulalong-
korn University, Thailand. She has a doctorate from Cambridge
University, has worked as an expert at the International Labour
Office, and has served as a Consultant for the World Bank and
Unesco. Her published works cover topics on labour, the service
sector, Japanese firms overseas, economic policy making, and
economic development.